Now that I'm a Christian

E.F.Kevan

 EVANGELICAL PRESS

EVANGELICAL PRESS
16/18 High Street, Welwyn, Hertfordshire. AL6 9EQ, England.

© Evangelical Press

First published by Evangelical Press 1975
Second impression 1978
Third impression 1982
Fourth impression 1983

ISBN 0 85234 071 0

Printed in the U.S.A.

CONTENTS

CHAPTER I

WHAT HAS HAPPENED?

You have been saved. But what does this mean? Saved from what? Saved for what? Is the word "saved" merely a piece of jargon used by preachers, or does it tell us anything? The answer is that the word is full of meaning; because until you were saved you were lost.

FIRST OF ALL YOU WERE LOST

This is the word that Christ uses Himself. Look it up in Luke 19, verse 10, where you will read, "The Son of man is come to seek and to save that which was lost". But what is a "lost" man when the word is used in this way? Our Lord told three stories which help us to understand this a little. They are all in chapter 15 of Luke's Gospel.

He first of all described a shepherd who had one hundred sheep, ninety-nine of which were safely in the fold, but one was "lost" (verses 4-6). It was away from him; it was no longer near him or available to him. But the sheep itself was destitute and hungry, possibly wounded. This is what it meant to be lost from the point of view of the sheep. In the same way, we whom the Saviour came to seek were lost to God; we were away from Him. Further, this meant that we were destitute, wounded by life, and perishing.

The second story, that of the lost coin (verses 8-9), indicates that a thing of value was no longer fulfilling its purpose. To be lost, therefore, means that the real worth of our life is not being realised.

The third story told by our Lord was of the lost son (verses 11-32), and this emphasises the particular meaning of the word "lost" which is more closely linked to human experience. The son was away from his father and his father's home. He was in the far country, and there, having wasted his substance with riotous living, he was in want, in rags, in degradation and in shame. He was destroying himself; all the noble qualities of human life and sonship were stripped from him. It is no wonder that in our Lord's story the father says, "He was lost". If we put these three stories together we gain some idea of what the Lord has saved us from. We were lost like this.

THE VALUE OF A PERSON

On another occasion our Lord put the challenging question, "What shall it profit a man, if he shall gain the whole world, and lose his own soul?" (Mark 8: 36). The word soul here means the *self*, and it shows that whilst a man can collect a great amount of material goods, he can lose "himself". This is further explained in the New Testament where a lost man is described as "having no hope, and without God in the world" (Ephesians 2: 12).

All this is summed up in an exceedingly expressive word in the famous sentence in John 3: 16. Here we are told that the purpose for which God sent His Son into the world was that those who believed in Him should not "perish". We cannot fully tell what the awfulness of perishing is, but it must be understood by us to be a sufficiently grave and serious experience as to justify the immense sacrifice that the Son of God was prepared to make in order that we should not "perish".

A SINNER

It is quite clear by now that behind this picture-word

8

"lost" we have the ugly realities of sin. It is by our sin that we become lost to God and lost to ourselves. Sin shuts us out from God. This is the meaning of the story that you find in the first book of the Bible, where Adam and Eve for their sin were expelled from the Garden of Eden. Sin shuts us off from all that is blessed and sweet. Sin hardens the conscience. Sin enslaves the man, bringing him into bondage so that he cannot truly reach the end for which he was made. Sin is the source of pain and sorrow, loneliness and death.

NEW LIFE

It is from all this that you have been saved. A little later on we shall see what Christ's work has to do with this, but first of all we may concentrate on answering the question with more regard to "what has happened". You have been born again (John 3: 7). Nothing less than this amazing and miraculous thing has happened to you. You were dead in sins and God by His Spirit has brought you to life (Ephesians 2: 1). You were in darkness, but God has opened your eyes and brought you into His light (1 Peter 2: 9). You have become what Paul calls a "new creature" (2 Corinthians 5: 17). By this supernatural action of God you have been wakened up from the sleep of sin and stirred to pray and to seek God.

YOU HAVE REPENTED

One of the ways in which praying and seeking for God expresses itself is in repentance. Repentance is a duty which God commands. John the Baptist prepared the way for Christ in the hearts of men by preaching that all men should repent (Matthew 3: 2). The early Christian preachers declared that God "commandeth all men everywhere to repent" (Acts 17: 30). You have repented, that is to say, you have experienced a change of mind and you have now turned your back on sin and sinning, and you have turned your face towards God. This is what has happened.

Not only have you repented, but you have come to believe. The Gospel is presented to those who are aware of their need, and faith is the act by which you have taken hold of it and committed yourself to the Saviour. You have entrusted yourself to Him, and have acknowledged that you cannot do anything to save yourself, but that you depend entirely on Him.

This experience of God by which you have been born again, and which expresses itself in repentance and faith, is often summarised by the word "conversion". Perhaps you have not met the word "conversion" very much in your previous thinking, but it means exactly what the word says. You have been turned round. You are no longer walking in the old way: you are looking in a new direction. In a later chapter we shall be able to study the meaning of this word more fully, but for the time being it is the word that explains in so many ways "what has happened".

FORGIVENESS

One of the wonderful things in your life is that you have received the forgiveness of sins. In your repentance you confessed that you were a sinner and you acknowledged that sin stood in the way between God and yourself. When you trusted in Christ, however, you trusted His promise that He would receive you and forgive you. In the light of this experience of the Lord, it is possible for you to know that you are a forgiven person. Paul described his own salvation by saying, "I obtained mercy" (1 Timothy 1: 13). It is this same sort of mercy that you, too, have received, and God for Christ's sake has forgiven you (Ephesians 4: 32).

THE LORD JESUS CHRIST IS YOUR SAVIOUR

This last quotation of Scripture leads us on to an exceedingly important—indeed all-important—thing in what has happened. Everything that has happened to you in the way of salvation has come to you for Christ's sake, that is to say, it depends upon what Christ has done for you. What Christ has done we can never fully tell, but in His death on the Cross He was actually taking the place which was yours, receiving Himself the reward due to your own sinful actions, and thus dying for you and in your place. His death releases you from the consequences of your sins.

The fruit of all this in your experience has been the peace of God. "We have peace with God through our Lord Jesus Christ" (Romans 5: 1). This peace may not be a highly emotional experience, but it will show itself in your conscience and in the quiet conviction that because you are trusting in Christ you may know that you are accepted by Him. From this sense of peace there also comes an experience of the Lord's power to overcome the temptations to sin which you will meet in the course of your Christian life. We shall talk more about this in another chapter.

Let us finish just now by reminding ourselves, as we did at the beginning, that a man is either lost or saved, and this all depends on his relation to the Lord Jesus Christ who alone is the Saviour.

CHAPTER 2

*Big things have happened in your experience, but perhaps you
are tempted to ask,*

HOW CAN I BE SURE?

Do you notice the form of the question? It does not ask
how I can *feel* sure, but how I can *be* sure. Christian experience is not a matter of simply feeling this or feeling that.
Christian experience is reality. It has to do with the verb
"to be", and so we may rightly ask, "How can I *be* sure?"

How foolish we are when we look on assurance as if it
were just a matter of the emotions! The emotions are as
insecure and changeful as the treacherous sandbanks under
the surface of the ocean. They are constantly forming and
reforming and afford no security whatever. There is an old
rhyme that runs,

> It is written!
> It is written!
> Here I rest my faith;
> Not on thoughts,
> And not on feelings,
> But on what He saith.

THE SOURCE OF ASSURANCE

These words at once direct us to the true source of security
and assurance. It is found not in ourselves, but in what God
has said and in what God has done.

It is important, therefore, that our confidence is put

in the right place. There are those who have invested their money in business concerns which they "felt" were secure, but which proved in due time not to be so.

If it is a serious matter in the ordinary affairs of life that our confidence should be well grounded, how much more important it is that in the eternal affairs of our spiritual destiny our confidence shall be in the right place.

WHERE ASSURANCE IS "NOT" FOUND

Granting, then, that our faith is in God—what then? You have prayed; you have read the Bible; you have done as the evangelist or Bible Class leader or minister has told you. But still you ask, "How can I be sure?"

Let us deal with this question first of all negatively. Our being sure does not depend on what we are. "All our righteousnesses are as filthy rags," says the prophet (Isaiah 64: 6). We dare not trust in ourselves. We cannot be sure, for example, on the ground of any new resolution we have firmly made; nor can we find any assurance in the joy that we are experiencing at this very moment.

Secondly, we cannot find our assurance in anything that we hope to become. It is gloriously true that God is able to make all grace abound toward us (2 Corinthians 9: 8), and we may therefore confidently hope that by His help we shall become the men and the women we long to be, but it is not on our prospects of improvement that we may base our present assurance.

Again, we cannot find assurance in anything that we are trying to do. This is what Paul meant when he said that "by the deeds of the law there shall no flesh be justified" (Romans 3: 20). To Jewish readers of Paul's letter, doing the "works of the law" meant the slavish obedience to the practices of Jewish religion. Those particular practices may have no appeal to us today, but many of us still possess the same slavish spirit as we try to put our confidence in our religious endeavours and intentions.

14

After all these negatives, I think you are beginning to see that the real positive truth is that we are to look away from ourselves and to trust only in the Lord Jesus Christ. The famous preacher, C. H. Spurgeon, has a beautiful illustration of this in one of his books. Picturesquely, he describes it like this. "I looked to the Lord, and the dove of peace flew into my breast. I looked at the dove, and it flew away."

Can you see Spurgeon's point? It is this. Only while we are looking to Christ in the simplicity of a childlike trust do we have peace. As soon, however, as we start looking at our peace, testing ourselves with a kind of morbid introspection, and wondering whether we are this or whether we are that, we lose our peace—the dove flies away. This is the "blessed assurance", as the hymn says: "Jesus is mine." Everything is in the Lord Jesus; it is all in what He has done, by the bearing away of your sin and in giving to you His own righteousness so that you are accepted by God on account of all that He is.

These two things, to which we give the words "Atonement" and "Justification", respectively, are the strong rock on which you can build your assurance. (In a later chapter we shall study a lot more about these two great words.)

GOD'S UNBREAKABLE PROMISE

The thing which we must not allow to slip out of our minds is that God has given us a promise. God is faithful. He cannot deny Himself. It is from that promise that all our assurance springs. If you ask me on what grounds I am sure of my own salvation today, I would reply that it is simply and solely because, having felt and acknowledged my need as a sinner, I came in faith to the Saviour whose promise is "Him that cometh to me I will in no wise cast out" (John 6: 37). That is what makes me sure. I expect God spoke some promise to you at the time when you found the Saviour. Go back to that promise again and again.

15

In a way that seems to supplement all this, we have what the New Testament calls the witness of the Holy Spirit in our hearts. Paul says, "The Spirit himself beareth witness with our spirit, that we are the children of God" (Romans 8: 16). This is a matter of experience, and only those who have experienced this can know its meaning. It is impossible for anyone of us to describe to a blind person what beautiful colours are like. It is impossible for us to explain to a born deaf person what beautiful sounds are like. These things must either be seen or heard to be known. It is because of this testimony of the Holy Spirit in our hearts, through the written word of God, that we possess a deep, and possibly quite unemotional, conviction that "I am His and He is mine".

This witness of the Spirit in our hearts is something quite other than a "glow" or "thrill" of which some people seem too easily to speak. We are nowhere promised "thrills", though it certainly is true that sometimes an awareness of the love of God overwhelms us. This inward testimony of God's Spirit is called, in 1 John 2: 27, by the name "anointing". That is a symbolical way of speaking of the work of the Holy Spirit in the heart. The verse reads: "But the anointing which ye have received of him abideth in you, and ye need not that any man teach you: but as the same anointing teacheth you of all things, and is truth, and is no lie, and even as it hath taught you, ye shall abide in him." Notice especially that John says that this anointing that we have of God "is truth, and is no lie".

BELIEVE YOUR BELIEFS

I remember coming across a saying on one occasion that ran like this: "Believe your beliefs and doubt your doubts; but do not doubt your beliefs or believe your doubts." I think there is a great amount of good common sense in this. When I was a boy seeking the assurance of salvation for my own heart, I remember speaking with an old lady who had been a Christian for many, many years. She was able to read my boyish heart like an open book. In reply to her questions I told her that my position was that if only I could "feel" saved I would then be able to believe in the Saviour. To which she so wisely and promptly replied that I was putting the cart before the horse. The Scripture says that we have "joy and peace in believing" (Romans 15: 13). Keep your assurance rightly grounded.

CHAPTER 3

Our salvation is from

THE EVIL CALLED SIN

It is an old riddle to ask which came first, "the chicken or the egg?" A similar problem perplexes many with regard to the origin of evil. There are two kinds of evil: one we call physical (or natural) evil, that is to say, evil that belongs to the physical world, the world of nature; the other we call moral evil, that is to say, evil which exists in the minds and motives, feelings and thoughts of man.

Which came first? Some would have us believe that physical or natural evil came first. They hold that moral evil, or what we call sin, arises out of man's misfortunes and difficulties in battling with his evil environment. The Bible, however, puts the matter the other way round. It tells us that when God made all things He pronounced them "good" (Genesis 1: 31).

THE ENTRY OF SIN INTO THE WORLD

It was a fair and beautiful world indeed as it left the Creator's hands, and into this lovely world God placed man. Man, too, was declared by God to be very good. The first trace that we have of anything to mar the perfection of God's handiwork is when the Evil One instils rebellion and distrust into man's mind. Man is led first to doubt the good faith of his Maker, and then to disobey the Creator's will. This, of course, is moral evil, or sin. The evil called sin has arrived! But it is an intruder, having no proper place in the universe that God has made.

With the entry of sin came sorrow, suffering, degeneration and death. The purpose of this Bible story of the commencement of things is not merely to satisfy our intellectual curiosity about the beginning of the world, but to bring home to us this serious and important truth that sin is an enemy, sin is unnatural, and sin is the root of all bitterness, pain and death. We now have the answer to our question. Moral evil—the evil called sin—came first, and it brought all natural evils in its train.

THE FACT OF SIN

The fact of "sin" cannot now be denied. There was a time when the general opinion about sin was optimistic. At the turn of the last century there were many people who felt that sin was on its way out. Two world wars, however, with the diabolical things that came with those wars, have exploded that myth entirely. Whatever else the optimistic philosopher may wish to say about sin, he certainly cannot carry conviction in the minds of his listeners when he tries to persuade them that sin does not exist.

There is all too much evidence of sin. Sin is one of the inescapable problems of human thought and experience. The wonderful glory of the Christian Gospel is that it faces this grim fact and shows the way of deliverance from sin. Other forms of religion either ignore the reality of sin or are baffled by it: the loving power of God in Christ saves from it (Romans 6: 6).

WHAT SIN IS

What, then, is this evil called sin? We have already seen that it does not belong to the world as God made it. It is a blot that has come upon all creation, and more particularly upon the human race.

One of the best ways of examining this evil called sin is to learn a little about the words that the Bible uses to describe it. The most common of these words contains the idea of "missing the mark", or "coming short" in some way. It has to do with the idea of aiming at a target and failing to hit it, or with the idea of a thing that is weighed in the balances and is insufficient.

Another word which gives a great deal of light on the subject is one which is frequently translated in our Bible by the word "transgression". To transgress means, literally, to cross over a line, and so "transgression" in the Bible sense is to cross the boundary-line of God's holy Law and to step into forbidden ground. Transgression springs from the spirit of rebellion or revolt. It contains the element of a refusal of subjection to right authority. It is law-breaking.

The last of the important words which we must notice is one which represents the idea of a wrong attitude. It is sometimes translated by the word "iniquity" in our Bible. It means perversion, distortion, or crookedness. A thing that is crooked is out of the straight, and this is exactly what the word "unrighteous" means. This third term, there-fore, describes not so much the action of sin, but the state of one who sins.

If you turn to the Bible in Psalm 32: 1 and 2, you will find all three words repeated. The Psalmist says, "Blessed is he whose transgression (rebellion) is forgiven, whose sin (missing the mark) is covered. Blessed is the man unto whom the Lord imputeth not iniquity (perversion of heart)".

In addition to these words, there are a great many others suggesting the ideas of evil disposition, irreverence, contempt of law, depravity, and the desire for what is forbidden.

Putting all these things together, we see that sin is a coming short of God's standard through an act of will which in turn issues in a permanent state. Let us understand at this point quite clearly, then, that sin is not a calamity that, having come upon man unawares, now spoils his happiness; rather it is an evil course which man has deliberately chosen to follow and which carries untold misery with it. It is not something passive, like a weakness, or a simple imperfection, but something active and opposed to God.

EVERYBODY HAS SINNED

Sin is universal. There is no one who has not sinned. This is the testimony of every sensitive conscience, but it is also the statement of Scripture. "All have sinned, and come short of the glory of God" (Romans 3: 23). In an earlier verse in this chapter, Paul quotes from the Psalms: "There is none righteous, no, not one" (Psalm 14: 3; Romans 3: 10). All the world is "become guilty before God" (Romans 3: 19).

THREE SERIOUS CONSEQUENCES OF SIN

Sin involves those who commit it in three serious consequences.

DEPRAVITY

The first of these is depravity. The heart is corrupted by sin. "The imagination of man's heart is evil from his youth" (Genesis 8: 21). Again, "The wicked are estranged from the womb: they go astray as soon as they be born, speaking lies" (Psalm 58: 3). David confesses, "Behold, I was shapen in iniquity; and in sin did my mother conceive me" (Psalm 51: 5). The ugly truth is announced by Jeremiah that "the heart is deceitful above all things, and desperately wicked" (Jeremiah 17: 9).

All of these passages have been found in the Old Testament, but if you will study the New Testament you will find the same truth is there emphasised. This word depravity is perhaps a little terrifying, but how truly terrifying sin is. In one of its aspects "depravity" stands for the lack of that original uprightness and purity in which man was made. It has a deeper meaning, however, in that it

22

•

indicates a terrible bias towards evil by which all man's actions are made spiritually worthless. When speaking of the "depravity" of man, we do not mean that every man is as bad as bad can be, for there are very many fine people about who make no profession of religion at all. These very fine people, however, would have to be described by Paul as "having the understanding darkened, being alienated from the life of God" (Ephesians 4: 18). An unconverted man or woman is destitute of that love to God which constitutes the very essence of true holiness. In place of this he is possessed by an aversion to God, which, though sometimes passive within him, occasionally bursts forth into active enmity as soon as God's will comes into conflict with his own. Our Lord confirmed this fact of the inwardness of sin by what He had to say about the evil heart (Mark 7: 21-23).

GUILT

The second consequence of sin is guilt. This means two things. First, that the sinner is personally unworthy. It is what we might call demerit or shame. The second aspect is liability to punishment. The broken Law needs solemn and holy vindication, and those who violate it receive what Paul calls "the wages of sin" (Romans 6: 23). There are, of course, differences of guilt. This depends on the amount of light and knowledge the wrongdoer has previously been given, but, when all these variations of guilt are allowed for, it still remains true that so far as the fact of guilt is concerned, "there is no difference" (Romans 3: 22).

PENALTY

The third aspect of the consequence of sin is penalty. Penalty is more than the merely unfortunate results that follow from making mistakes. It is the act of the Divine Law-Giver and Judge. It is this that leads to "condemnation". The purpose of punishment is not the reformation of the sinner, nor the prevention of others from doing wrong, but definitely and positively to vindicate the claims of the Law itself. The punishment of sin is experienced in its beginnings in this life, but the ultimate punishment is that of eternity.

This is the evil called sin. It is no wonder, therefore, that when Paul asks, "Shall we continue in sin, that grace may abound?" he exclaims, "God forbid" (Romans 6: 1, 2).

CHAPTER 4

In this chapter we try to learn something about

THE SAVIOUR WE KNOW

If we were thinking of an ordinary person we would usually start by describing his parents and the home in which he was born. When we come to think of our Saviour, however, we must go back much farther because—as we shall see presently—He is both God and man.

THE MYSTERY OF GOD

Our thoughts on the Person of Christ, then, must begin with a right understanding of the nature of God Himself. Here we meet with truths which are quite beyond the power of our reasoning. It is impossible to "explain" God. He is revealed to us, however, and this is where we Christians begin. The Bible reveals Him as God the Father, God the Son, and God the Holy Spirit. We commonly speak of this as the Holy Trinity. The Lord Jesus Christ is God the Son, and we read in the Scriptures that "the Father sent the Son to be the Saviour of the world" (1 John 4: 14).

THE INCARNATION

At Christmas time we celebrate the coming of the Son of God into human life. This is what is meant by the Incarnation. It means "God became man". It is the truth which underlies the title which we sometimes give to Christ. "Emmanuel"—"God with us" (Matthew 1: 23). The Incarnation was the realisation of this sacred mission which the Father entrusted to His Son.

The coming of Christ into the world was by a miracle. His mother, Mary, was a young woman upon whom God came by the gentle power of His Holy Spirit, working miraculously within her body, so that she became the mother of a child. This is the fact that we usually indicate when we speak of the virgin birth of our Lord. The stories of our Lord's birth in this supernatural way are most delicately given to us in Matthew 1: 18-25, and Luke 1: 5 to 2: 20.

You should read these stories, and especially note the following words: "And the angel said unto her, Fear not, Mary: for thou hast found favour with God. And, behold, thou shalt conceive in thy womb, and bring forth a son, and shalt call his name JESUS. He shall be great, and shall be called the Son of the Highest: and the Lord God shall give unto him the throne of his father David: and he shall reign over the house of Jacob for ever; and of his kingdom there shall be no end. Then said Mary unto the angel, How shall this be, seeing I know not a man? And the angel answered and said unto her, The Holy Ghost shall come upon thee, and the power of the Highest shall overshadow thee: therefore also that holy thing which shall be born of thee shall be called the Son of God" (Luke 1: 30-35).

When we read the Gospels we find that the record of the life and ministry of Christ fully bears out this truth that He is both God and man.

WHAT OUR LORD SAID ABOUT HIMSELF

We might perhaps first of all notice what our Lord said about Himself. If we turn to Luke's Gospel we find the story in chapter 2 of a visit which our Lord paid to the temple at the age of twelve. When His parents found Him in the temple and rebuked Him, our Lord gave the astonishing reply, "How is it that ye sought me? wist ye not that I must be about my Father's business?" (Luke 2: 49). It is clear from these words that quite early in our Lord's human life He knew Himself to stand in a special relation to God as His Father.

The sense of a special relation to the Father is found throughout the Saviour's entire life and teaching. He says, rather arrestingly, in Matthew 11: 27, "All things are delivered unto me of my Father: and no man knoweth the Son, but the Father; neither knoweth any man the Father, save the Son, and he to whomsoever the Son will reveal him". When our Lord was in dispute with the Jews, He said to them, "Ye are from beneath; I am from above: ye are of this world; I am not of this world" (John 8: 23). One of the most remarkable sayings of our Lord is to be found in John 16: 28, which reads: "I came forth from the Father, and am come into the world: again, I leave the world, and go to the Father."

OUR LORD'S DIVINE ACTIONS

All that our Lord said in this connection is supported by the things that He did. For example, our Lord readily accepted the worship that was offered to Him by men. This happened after the stilling of the storm (Matthew 14: 33), and after the healing of the blind man (John 9: 38). He accepted it from the Canaanitish woman (Matthew 15: 25), and from Thomas after the Resurrection (John 20: 28). More than this, one of the most familiar features of the Gospel story is the way in which our Lord exercised the Divine right to forgive sins. You will see this in Mark 2: 1-12, and in John 8: 1-11. These and many other features in the Gospel story make it quite plain to us that our Lord was more than man.

27

OUR LORD WAS TRULY MAN

At the same time, we must not lose sight of the fact that He was truly man. He shared our physical experiences. He knew what it was to be tired and to be hungry. He knew our mental experiences and "increased in wisdom" (Luke 2: 46-52). He entered into our sorrows and knew the deep troubles of our hearts. You will find much of this in John 12: 27 and Mark 14: 33, 34, for example.

Our Lord chose a special title for Himself. You will perhaps remember that this was the title "Son of Man". See this especially in such a verse as Luke 19: 10. Our Saviour was true and complete in His manhood, and all those who met with Him, both friends and foes alike, had no doubt whatever that this was so.

THE TEACHING OF THE NEW TESTAMENT

When we turn from the Gospels to the other writings of the New Testament—that is, the Epistles—we find it all the more plain that our Lord was truly God. His great title "The Lord Jesus Christ", emphasises the outstanding truth about His person and work. The name "Jesus", of course, is that which refers to His human life and reminds us also of His purpose in coming to be our "Saviour". The title "Christ" speaks of Him as God's "Anointed" King who came in fulfilment of Old Testament promise and prophecy. When, however, He is spoken of as "The Lord", we are directed at once to His nature as God. In 1 Corinthians 12: 3, we have a kind of Christian confession which it would appear was made by early believers when they became Christians. It is "Jesus is the Lord".

In Romans 9: 5, the Saviour is called "God blessed for ever", and in Titus 2: 13 (R.V.), Paul describes Him as "our great God and Saviour Jesus Christ". Hebrews 4: 14, speaks of the great High Priest whom believers have, and names Him as "Jesus the Son of God". If you turn to 1 John 4: 14 and 15, you will see this truth even more firmly asserted. Our Lord is described in Colossians 1: 16-17, as the Creator of all things, while in Philippians 2: 5-8, Paul describes our Lord as being "in the form of God", that is to say, possessing all those personal properties that belong to God.

EVIDENCE FROM THE RESURRECTION

The resurrection of the Lord Jesus was one of the greatest and most powerful evidences that He was God. Paul reasons in this way in Romans 1: 4, when he says that though Christ was made of the seed of David according to the flesh, He was powerfully declared to be the Son of God "by the resurrection from the dead". One of the most convincing aspects of this testimony is the fact that our Lord prophesied that He would rise again. See John 10: 18, and the significant phrase, "as he said", in Matthew 28: 6. Our Saviour is God Himself, Lord of life and death. No wonder Thomas exclaimed, "My Lord and My God"! (John 20: 28).

CHAPTER 5

Almost the last words spoken by our Lord on the Cross were,
"It is finished". We must now endeavour to understand

WHAT CHRIST HAS DONE

Our Lord came into the world to do something. In anticipation of this triumphant cry uttered by Him on the Cross,
there is a prophetic Psalm which, as it were, puts words
into the mouth of Christ and says, "Lo, I come . . . I
delight to do thy will, O my God" (Psalm 40: 7, 8).
Speaking to His disciples on one occasion, He said, "I do
always those things that please him" (John 8: 29). In His
prayer before going to His suffering and death, our Lord
said to His Father in heaven, "I have glorified thee on the
earth: I have finished the work which thou gavest me to
do" (John 17: 4). These words were spoken, of course, in
anticipation of the completed work on the Cross.

A SAVING WORK

We now, therefore, give our attention to the study of
what Christ has done. On one occasion our Lord said, "The
Son of man is come to seek and to save that which was
lost" (Luke 19: 10). This introduces us to the great feature
of our Lord's work. He had come to save. This was the
reason why He bore the name "Jesus" (see Matthew 1: 21).

In order to save us, our Lord first of all entered into
human life. He became a partaker of flesh and blood "that

31

through death he might destroy him that had the power of death, that is, the devil" (Hebrews 2: 14). He lived a life of perfection and goodness. He is described by Paul in 2 Corinthians 5: 21, as Him who "knew no sin", and the purpose of this was that He might offer Himself in death, the "just for the unjust" (1 Peter 3: 18). On the third day He rose from the dead and subsequently ascended up where He was before. The whole story of our Lord's work is expressed in the most concise language of John 16: 28: "I came forth from the Father, and am come into the world: again, I leave the world, and go to the Father". In His coming into the world, in what He did while He was here, and in His victorious departure from the world is comprised much of the saving work of Christ.

There can be no doubt, however, that in the New Testament the central emphasis is placed upon our Lord's death on the Cross. The death of Christ on the Cross is mentioned nearly two hundred times in the New Testament. Our Lord's birth and His life lead up to the Cross; and His resurrection and ascension have their meaning because of it. It is for this clear reason that Paul exclaimed, "God forbid that I should glory, save in the cross of our Lord Jesus Christ" (Galatians 6: 14).

Let us enquire a little more into the meaning of our Lord's saving work on the Cross.

SACRIFICE

First of all, we find language in the Bible that speaks of our Lord's work as a "sacrifice". John the Baptist introduced the Saviour to his disciples by announcing, "Behold the Lamb of God, which taketh away the sin of the world" (John 1: 29). The next day he used the same phrase—"the Lamb of God"—a second time concerning the Saviour. For your own inspiration and instruction count up in the book of Revelation and see how many times Jesus is called "the Lamb".

This title takes us back to the Old Testament, where sacrifice was ordained by God for His people as the way by which sin could be put away. Look up the references to this in Leviticus, chapters 1 to 7, and study especially the whole of chapter 16. We now know, of course, that there was no value in those sacrifices in themselves, but that they were being used by God to point on to His own Son who by offering Himself as the substitute for the sinner would be the means of his salvation and restoration to God.

THE EPISTLE TO THE HEBREWS

Turn now to Hebrews, chapter 9. Stop your reading of this book for a few moments and study this passage most carefully. Note especially verses 9-14, "which was a figure for the time then present, in which were offered both gifts and sacrifices, that could not make him that did the service perfect, as pertaining to the conscience; which stood only in meats and drinks, and divers washings, and carnal ordinances, imposed on them until the time of reformation. But Christ being come an high priest of good things to come, by a greater and more perfect tabernacle, not made with hands, that is to say, not of this building; neither by the blood of goats and calves, but by his own blood he entered in once into the holy place, having obtained eternal redemption for us. For if the blood of bulls and of goats, and the ashes of an heifer sprinkling the unclean, sanctifieth to the purifying of the flesh; how much more shall the blood of Christ, who through the eternal Spirit offered himself without spot to God, purge your conscience from dead works to serve the living God?"

ISAIAH CHAPTER 53

Returning to the Old Testament, open the Bible at Isaiah, chapter 53, and particularly pay attention to verses 5-7. It is plain that Isaiah is speaking prophetically about the Lord Jesus Christ in this place. "Brought as a lamb" is a clear allusion to the sacrifice and saving work of the Lord Jesus.

THE TORN VEIL

When the Lord Jesus died on the Cross, something re-markable happened. We are told in Matthew 27: 50 and 51, "Jesus, when he had cried again with a loud voice, yielded up the ghost. And, behold, the veil of the temple was rent in twain from the top to the bottom". In the days of Jewish religion, the veil in the temple, hanging between what was known as "the Holy Place" and "the Most Holy Place", represented the barrier which sin had made between God and man, and which needed to be removed by means of the offering of sacrifice. This Divine act in ripping apart the veil symbolised the fact that our Lord's death as the great sacrifice for sin had now opened the way into God's presence. This was surely what He meant when He said, "I am the way . . . no man cometh unto the Father but by me" (John 14: 6). All is now clear for the sinner to come to God. The result of this is seen in Hebrews 4: 16, and 10: 19-22, which you should now stop to read.

OUR LORD'S DEATH IS A RANSOM

Looking a little more into the New Testament, we find that our Lord's saving work is described as our "redemption". You will come upon this word in Ephesians 1: 7, "In whom we have redemption through his blood." To redeem means to set free by means of a ransom, that is, by the payment of a price. The action refers to the custom of slavery in the ancient world. A man had been sold into slavery and only by purchase could he be freed from it. You should now turn back to Matthew 20: 28, where you read, "the Son of man came . . . to give his life a ransom for many". The word "ransom", here, means a liberating price, and refers to the effects of the death of our Lord in setting free the sinner who has been bound by the chains of his own sin, and who is under condemnation. Read the words of the Saviour in John 8: 36: "If the Son therefore shall make you free, ye shall be free indeed."

In accomplishing this work of our salvation, which we have seen to be by the sacrifice of Himself and the giving of His own life as a ransom-price, our Lord put Himself in the sinner's place. This is what we mean by the word "substitution". Jesus substituted Himself for the sinner; He stood and suffered in the sinner's stead.

> O Christ, what burdens bowed Thy head!
> Our load was laid on Thee;
> Thou stoodest in the sinner's stead,
> Didst bear all ill for me.
> A Victim led, Thy blood was shed!
> Now there's no load for me.
>
> Death and the curse were in our cup:
> O Christ, 'twas full for Thee!
> But Thou hast drained the last dark drop,
> 'Tis empty now for me:
> That bitter cup, love drank it up,
> Now blessing's draught for me.

A striking incident took place at the time of our Lord's crucifixion and, though dramatic enough in itself, it seems to point beyond the immediate event and show what was really happening when our Lord went out to die. It was customary for the Roman authorities to show a favour to the Jews at the Passover season by releasing any political prisoner whom they cared to choose. A man named Barabbas was a notable criminal and prisoner at that time, and Pilate made an offer to the Jews to release either Jesus or Barabbas. "Away with this man, and release unto us Barabbas," was the frenzied cry of the crowd (Luke 23: 18), and so we read in Mark's Gospel, "Pilate . . . released Barabbas unto them, and delivered Jesus . . . to be crucified" (chapter 15, verse 15). By popular clamour and violation of justice Jesus stood in the place of Barabbas in a dramatic

35

exchange of position. This seems to indicate to us the very heart of the saving work of Christ.

John Bunyan depicts Christian in *The Pilgrim's Progress* as coming to the hill of Calvary and losing the burden of his sin. These are his delightful words:

"Now I saw in my dream, that the highway up which Christian was to go, was fenced on either side with a wall, and that wall was called Salvation. Up this way, therefore, did burdened Christian run, but not without great difficulty, because of the load on his back. He ran thus till he came at a place somewhat ascending; and upon that place stood a Cross, and a little below, in the bottom, a sepulchre. So I saw in my dream, that just as Christian came up with the Cross, his burden loosed from off his shoulders, and fell down off his back, and began to tumble, and so continued to do, till it came to the mouth of the sepulchre, where it fell in, and I saw it no more. Then was Christian glad and lightsome, and said with a merry heart, he hath given me rest by his sorrow, and life by his death. Then he stood still a while, to look and wonder, for it was very surprising to him that the sight of the cross should thus ease him of his burden. He looked, therefore, and looked again, even till the springs that were in his hand sent the waters down his cheeks. . . . Then Christian gave three leaps for joy, and went on singing,

'Thus far did I come laden with my sin,
Nor could ought ease the grief that I was in,
Till I came hither! What a place is this!
Must here be the beginning of my bliss?
Must here the burden fall from off my back?
Must here the strings that bound it to me crack?
Blest cross! blest sepulchre! blest rather be
The Man that there was put to shame for me!' "

THE FINISHED WORK OF CHRIST

It is customary for believers to say that they are trusting in "the finished work of Christ". This grand phrase refers to our Lord's sin-bearing death, and it stresses the truth that Christ has done "once for all" everything that is needful for our forgiveness and for our full salvation. Have you ever been tempted to think that you could do anything to supplement what Christ has done? Banish the thought! Christ has borne it all, done it all, and procured it all.

> I would not work my soul to save,
>   For that my Lord has done;
> But I would work like any slave
>   For love of God's dear Son.

CHAPTER 6

The Cross was not the end, and the Christian history confronts us with

THE GRAVE THAT IS EMPTY

The title of this chapter is put in these words because there is only one grave like this.

THE FACTS

The facts are as follows. The body of Jesus was taken down from the Cross by His sorrowing friends and was tenderly wrapped in linen and placed in a rock-hewn tomb belonging to a man named Joseph of Arimathaea (Luke 23 : 50-56). The Roman authorities saw to it that the great stone which made the door of the tomb was rolled heavily against the opening, and they sealed it with the seal of the Roman governor (Matthew 27 : 65, 66). In the morning of "the third day" after this, some of our Lord's friends paid a visit to the tomb, hoping for an opportunity to give further loving care to the precious body after its hurried burial. They were confronted with the startling sight of the tomb wide open and a heavenly visitor who said, "Fear not ye: for I know that ye seek Jesus, which was crucified. He is not here: for he is risen, as he said. Come, see the place where the Lord lay" (Matthew 28 : 5, 6). The grave was empty! This is the fact which has confounded unbelief and has satisfied faith for nearly twenty centuries.

Our Lord subsequently came to His followers and told them something of the meaning of this great event, and then commissioned them to go to every place and be witnesses of the resurrection (Luke 24: 47, 48). The apostle Peter began his preaching in this way: "Ye men of Israel, hear these words; Jesus of Nazareth, a man approved of God among you by miracles and wonders and signs, which God did by him in the midst of you, as ye yourselves also know: Him, being delivered by the determinate counsel and foreknowledge of God, ye have taken, and by wicked hands have crucified and slain: whom God hath raised up, having loosed the pains of death: because it was not possible that he should be holden of it" (Acts 2: 22-24). Peter pressed home the conclusion of all this by saying, "Therefore let all the house of Israel know assuredly, that God hath made that same Jesus, whom ye have crucified, both Lord and Christ" (Acts 2: 36).

The Lordship and Saviourhood of Jesus are exactly what follow from "the grave that is empty". This was His triumph.

INTELLECTUAL DIFFICULTIES

The Christians at Corinth—a great Greek city of New Testament days—were being troubled by rationalistic arguments and philosophical questions that seemed to confuse their minds on the subject of the resurrection. There were all kinds of problems connected with it. And there still are! For no one has all the answers from a scientific point of view. But the one piece of undeniable evidence for the resurrection is the fact of "the grave that is empty". This is the fact that Paul brings to these perplexed Corinthian Christians. He confronts all the theoretical prejudice against the possibility of the resurrection of the dead by saying, "But now is Christ risen from the dead" (1 Corinthians 15: 20).

THOSE WHO SAW HIM ALIVE

Paul states the resurrection of Christ as a fact for which there is all-sufficient evidence. He enumerates some of this in the opening part of his great chapter on the resurrection —1 Corinthians 15. It is my teaching, he says, that Christ died for our sins according to the Scriptures, and that He was buried, and that He rose again the third day. He then adds the testimony for the resurrection. Our Lord was seen by Peter (verse 5), by the twelve (verse 5), by a company of 500, many of whom were still living at the time of Paul's writing and could endorse what he was saying (verse 6), by James (verse 7), and then by all the apostles (verse 7). To all this evidence Paul adds his own, that he, too, had seen the Lord (verse 8).

THE HISTORY IN THE BOOK OF THE ACTS

This book was written by Luke some time between the years A.D. 63 and the Fall of Jerusalem in A.D. 70. He tells us in the preface to his Gospel that he had gathered his information from eye-witnesses. This, we may conclude, was also the way in which he prepared the book of the Acts. Further, as certain sections in the history show—by the use of the pronoun "we"—Luke was a participator in some of the events which he narrates. He was right in the midst of the early preaching, and took a share in the great happenings of the early days.

FIRST-HAND EVIDENCE

We have in Luke, therefore, a contemporary and first-hand witness, one also who has been proved by historical criticism to be both conscientious and accurate. Further, it is impossible to suppose that the Early Church did not know its own history; and the very fact of the acceptance by the Early Church of this book is evidence of its accuracy and truth.

When we read the story of these early days, as the book gives it to us, we learn that the resurrection of Christ was the perpetual theme of the apostolic preaching, and that the apostolic Church was brought into being on the fact of the risen Christ. One careful writer has said, "As the Church is too holy for a foundation of rottenness, so she is too real for a foundation of mist". An impartial examination of this history of the Early Church reveals that everything centred in one great event, and that was the resurrection of Jesus Christ. In its joyful existence, in its faith, in its preaching, in its ordinances, and in its immediate obervance of the Lord's Day, the Church revealed that its very existence was evidence that Jesus had risen from the dead.

HOW TO START A "NEW RELIGION"

The following story is told of a conversation which occurred at the time of the French Revolution. One of the leaders complained to Talleyrand that it was so hard to start a new religion. "Sure," said Talleyrand, "it cannot be as difficult as you think." "How so?" said his friend. "Why," he replied, "the matter is simple. You have only to get yourself crucified or anyhow put to death, and then, at your own time, to rise from the dead, and you will have no difficulty." We may endorse the Frenchman's subtle answer, and thus find ourselves affirming again that nothing less than the actual rising again from the dead of our Lord Jesus Christ could possibly account for the transformation of the disciples and the faith of the Christian Church.

WHAT THE GOSPELS HAVE TO SAY

In the first three Gospels we have written evidence which belongs to a date some seven or eight years earlier than the book of the Acts. The testimony of these Gospels comes in this way from those who were participants in the history, and it belongs to a period separated from the event by no more than thirty years. What the testimony of the Gospels is everybody knows.

THE DISCOVERY OF THE RESURRECTION

The records tell how Jesus Christ, having been crucified

and buried, was discovered early in the morning on the first day of the week to have risen from the dead. Visitors to the tomb found the stone rolled away, the tomb empty, and the Roman guard departed. Angels met the visitors with the question, "Why seek ye the living among the dead?" In addition, they volunteered the information, "He is not here, but is risen" (Luke 24: 5-6).

This amazing discovery at the tomb was followed by repeated encounters with the Lord Himself. In the meantime the Jewish and Roman authorities devised a tale by which to contradict the miracle (Matthew 28: 11-15). These narratives show that although our Lord had foretold His rising again—and the first three Gospels record it at least ten times—none of the disciples seem to have understood it, and certainly none of them expected it. Those who first discovered the fact were filled with the mixed emotions of "fear and great joy" (Matthew 28: 8), and some of the Lord's intimate circle could not at first believe it (Matthew 28: 17).

OBJECTIONS

Let us now turn to this question of credibility, for there have been those who have attacked the story as being impossible. The resurrection of Christ has been denied by the rationalists and by those who for other reasons are opposed to the Christian Gospel. A number of countersuggestions have been put forward in contradiction to the Christian evidence. Some have suggested that the whole thing is to be explained by the idea that the disciples stole the body of Jesus. Others invent the idea that our Lord never really died but only swooned on the Cross and later "came round". Others offer the suggestion that the appearances which are recorded in the Gospels were nothing other than hallucinations, and that the hysterical women and other friends of Jesus imagined they saw the Lord. Yet another view is that the whole idea of the resurrection was invented many years afterwards in order to give special support to the claims of the Christian Church.

In reply to all these we may perhaps use the words of James Orr: "None of these theories can stand examination. The objections are but small dust of the balance compared with the strength of the evidence for the fact. From the stand-point of faith, the resurrection of Jesus is the most credible of events. If Jesus was indeed such a one as the Gospel declares Him to be, it was impossible that death should hold Him."

Underlying all these alternative suggestions in contradiction of the fact of the resurrection of Christ, there is one great and fundamental denial. It is the denial that such a miracle could possibly have happened. This is most unscientific, however, for all science worthy of the name sets about in the first place to gather the facts and then to draw the conclusions from the facts. It is certainly an absurdity of thought to start off with a fixed opinion and then distort the facts to suit the opinion. It may be said at this point that there certainly is a tremendous presumption against the resurrection of any ordinary man. Indeed, it is most unlikely that any ordinary man should rise from the dead. But when we are confronted with Jesus, as He is portrayed in the Gospels, we must reverse the proposition and say of *this* man that it was impossible that He should not rise from the dead.

That the foes of Christ were not able effectively to deny the resurrection gives overwhelming strength to its credibility. If Jesus were still dead, then His enemies were powerful enough either to produce or to find His body. The fact that they did neither of these things brings confusion to all arguments that deny the resurrection.

THE IMPORTANCE OF THE RESURRECTION

The importance of the resurrection of Christ cannot be overstated. Our hope of salvation stands or falls with it.

This is the fact by which the entire structure of Christian doctrine and experience is held together. If this be removed, then everything else is removed; if this be proved untrue, then all else is proved untrue.

No statement of the issues involved can be clearer or more powerful than the words of Paul in 1 Corinthians 15: 14-19. "And if Christ be not risen, then is our preaching vain, and your faith is also vain. Yea, and we are found false witnesses of God; because we have testified of God that he raised up Christ: whom he raised not up, if so be that the dead rise not. For if the dead rise not, then is not Christ raised: and if Christ be not raised, your faith is vain; ye are yet in your sins. Then they also which are fallen asleep in Christ are perished. If in this life only we have hope in Christ, we are of all men most miserable."

Reasoning of this kind means to say that if the resurrection of Christ is not a fact, then Christianity is a delusion. But let it be said again, that at the heart of the Christian Gospel is the fact of "the grave that is empty".

CHAPTER 7

In our last four chapters we have been thinking about some of the facts connected with our salvation such as the nature of sin from which we need to be freed, and the love and work of our Saviour. In this chapter we look again into the meaning of our experience of salvation, and we begin with the

RIGHT ABOUT TURN

This is conversion. The necessity for conversion arises from the fact of sin. In one of his sermons, Spurgeon declared the necessity for a change of nature in a sinner by saying that if a thief went to heaven without it he would be a thief still and would go round the place picking the angels' pockets. The Mayor of Cambridge complained about Spurgeon's insufficient knowledge of angels, and remarked that angels did not have pockets. Whereupon the famous preacher made the amusing rejoinder at a subsequent service that the unconverted thief would "steal the feathers out of the angels' wings".

WHAT IS CONVERSION?

What happens in conversion? The old story is told of a clergyman who made several attempts to reform a bad character. Finally, the man sought to repulse him by making the remark, "It is all in vain, Sir: you cannot get me to change my religion". "I do not want that," replied the good man, "I wish religion to change you."

Conversion implies that we need to be turned round. This is the exact meaning of our English word. The truth about us is that our faces are turned in the wrong direction. We have turned away from God. By our sin we have turned our backs on God. Conversion, therefore, requires that this "turning" shall be made again, and we shall turn once more to God.

WHAT THE BIBLE SAYS

Let us examine some of the Bible passages. When men deny God in their hearts, that is to say, when they live as if God did not exist, they immediately become corrupt. This is what Psalm 14: 1 means where we read: "The fool hath said in his heart, There is no God. They are corrupt, they have done abominable works, there is none that doeth good."

Our sinful condition is described in Genesis 6: 5; "And God saw that the wickedness of man was great in the earth, and that every imagination of the thoughts of his heart was only evil continually". Psalm 94: 11 summarises God's estimate of the thoughts of man, "that they are vanity".

The same truth about our moral condition and our alienation from God is given in Isaiah 53: 6, and in Psalm 119: 176. These two verses tell us plainly that the trouble in our lives arises from the fact that we have chosen our own way.

OUR ENMITY AGAINST GOD

This choosing of our own path and turning of our backs on God is further described in the New Testament as enmity against God, or alienation from Him. Look at Romans 8: 7 and 8, and read the following words: "Because the carnal mind is enmity against God: for it is not subject to the law of God, neither indeed can be. So then they that are in the flesh cannot please God." (By the "carnal" mind Paul means the mind of a man that has not yet been renewed and brought into a right relation to God.)

The word "enmity" in this verse is exceedingly strong. In Romans 1: 30, there comes an even stronger expression, and Paul speaks of us in our unconverted state as being "haters of God". This is what James meant in James 4: 4, where he says "whosoever therefore will be a friend of the world is the enemy of God".

GOD'S GRACE OVERCOMES OUR ENMITY

Part of the purpose of our Lord's saving work is to make reconciliation. This is because, as Romans 5: 10, says, "we were enemies". We cannot escape this thought, for again in Colossians 1: 21, Paul writes: "And you, that were some-time alienated and enemies in your mind by wicked works, yet now hath he reconciled." The entire direction of our life until God turns us round is fully stated in Ephesians 2: 2: "In time past ye walked according to the course of this world, according to the prince of the power of the air, the spirit that now worketh in the children of disobedience."

A DARKENED UNDERSTANDING

This estrangement from God has its root and also its result in a clouding of our understanding. In Ephesians 4: 18, Paul describes sinful men as "having the understanding darkened, being alienated from the life of God through the ignorance that is in them, because of the blindness of their heart". See also 1 Corinthians 2: 14, and then especially turn to Romans 1: 18, where the apostle speaks of those who suppress knowledge of God in their consciences because of their wrongful desires. The Revised Version here speaks of the "ungodliness and unrighteousness of men, who hold down the truth in unrighteousness".

The Psalmist has a remark which seems to cover all these unpleasant features of sinful men when he describes them as those "that forget God" (Psalm 9: 17).

WE NEED TO TURN

The practice of sin has taught us to seek first ourselves and our own pleasure. This is the reason why the call from God to His sinning people through the prophets in the Old Testament was, "As I live, saith the Lord God, I have no pleasure in the death of the wicked; but that the wicked turn from his way and live: turn ye, turn ye from your evil ways; for why will ye die, O house of Israel?" (Ezekiel 33: 11). In the same prophecy at chapter 18, verse 30, God again says, "Repent, and turn yourselves from all your transgressions; so iniquity shall not be your ruin".

In Isaiah 1: 16 and 17, the prophet makes the same earnest exhortation in the name of God. "Wash you, make you clean; put away the evil of your doings from before mine eyes; cease to do evil; learn to do well." You are no doubt quite familiar already with the very well known words of God in Isaiah 55: 7: "Let the wicked forsake his way, and the unrighteous man his thoughts: and let him return unto the Lord, and he will have mercy upon him; and to our God, for he will abundantly pardon." From these words it is clear to see that if a man is truly to come to know God he must turn away from his sins and must turn toward God with a strong desire to know and to love Him.

OLD THINGS ARE PASSED AWAY

There are things to leave. John Bunyan tells us in the story of his life, which he entitles, *Grace Abounding*, that when he was still greatly burdened about his sins, though still finding it hard to break with the pleasures of them, he heard a voice which halted him. A voice, he says, "did suddenly dart from heaven into my soul, which said, 'Wilt thou leave thy sins and come to heaven, or have thy sins and go to hell?' At this I was put to an exceeding amaze". Bearing his own experience in mind, John Bunyan later on wrote, "If thou hast come, what hast thou come away from? What hast thou left behind? Hast thou left behind thy darling sins, thy vain pleasures and companions, thy pride and love of the world, thine own righteousness and self-pleasing? Take heed. If these things be in thy heart and life, why shouldest thou imagine thou art yet come to Jesus Christ?" Let us repeat it to ourselves: There are things to leave. A motorist paused and asked a country boy, "Will this road take me to London, lad?" To which the youth replied, "Yes, if you turn and go the other way".

WE ARE COMMANDED TO REPENT

The command to repent is repeated again and again. We have seen some of these in the Old Testament, but this is likewise the emphasis of the New. John the Baptist insisted upon it. When our Lord began preaching, He started on the same note (Matthew 4: 17). Later He sent out His disciples, "and they went out, and preached that men should repent" (Mark 6: 12). When Peter proclaimed the "Good News" on the Day of Pentecost, his first word in reply to the anxious questions of the people was "Repent" (Acts 2: 38).

WHAT IS REPENTANCE?

Perhaps at this point we ought to define more carefully what the word repent means. It has a number of elements in its meaning. Primarily it contains the idea of sorrowing or grieving about what one has done. It then means—and this is more particularly the New Testament meaning— "to change one's mind". Repentance therefore includes the double thought of sorrow over sin and the definite resolve to forsake it.

Realising how sinful he is and how unequal and unable for this "turning" he is, the Psalmist cries, "Turn us again, O God, and cause thy face to shine; and we shall be saved" (Psalm 80: 3). We find the same thought in Lamentations 5: 21: "Turn thou us unto thee, O Lord, and we shall be turned; renew our days as of old."

WE OWE OUR CONVERSION TO GOD'S MERCY

This last prayer puts us in a position to examine the subject of conversion more closely. We have to go behind it, and when we do so we once more come upon the gracious and merciful action of God. The more we learn about the way of salvation, the more we discover that God is first in everything. Long before we seek Him, He has been seeking us, and, as John so beautifully puts it, "We love him, because he first loved us" (1 John 4: 19). In closer connection with the subject of our repentance, look up the words in Acts 5: 30 and 31, and Acts 11: 18, where you will discover that repentance, even though it is our own action, is a gift from God, that is to say, it is something which God's Holy Spirit enables us to do.

THE NEW BIRTH

This merciful action of God that lies behind repentance and conversion is what we call "regeneration". Regeneration is the work of God. It is brought about by the life-giving Holy Spirit. As the very word suggests, it is the giving again of life. We are "dead" in trespasses and sins (Ephesians 2: 1).

> Lord, I was dead, I could not stir
> My lifeless soul to come to Thee;
> But now since Thou hast quickened me,
> I rise from sin's dark sepulchre.

One of the Old Testament ways of promising this great blessing is found in Ezekiel 36: 26 and 27: "A new heart also will I give you, and a new spirit will I put within you: and I will take away the stony heart out of your flesh, and I will give you an heart of flesh. And I will put my Spirit within you, and cause you to walk in my statutes, and ye shall keep my judgments, and do them." By nature we are as Paul describes us in 1 Corinthians 2: 14. He says, "The natural man receiveth not the things of the Spirit of God: for they are foolishness unto him: neither can he know them, because they are spiritually discerned". In view of this it is the work of God's Holy Spirit in us to bring about what Paul elsewhere calls the "renewing of your mind" (Romans 12: 2).

Our Lord spoke about this important work of renewal of heart and life in His conversation with Nicodemus. During the course of this, He told him plainly that it was necessary for a man to be born again if he were to hope to enter into the kingdom of God (John 3: 3-8).

EVIDENCE THAT A MAN HAS BEEN BORN AGAIN

How God works in the miracle of regeneration we do not know. It is an act as mysterious as creation itself. This is why Paul says to the Corinthians, "If any man be in Christ, he is a new creature" (2 Corinthians 5: 17). But although we cannot explain how God does His saving work in this respect, we are not without evidence that He has so worked. Regeneration brings about a new attitude to God, to oneself, and to all else. It effects a complete alteration in a man's way of life.

A SUMMARY

We have now assembled many of the things that together make up the experience called conversion. For the purpose of our study, we have had to distinguish between these things, but though distinguishable they are quite inseparable. Regeneration is never found without its manifestation in repentance and faith, and there is never repentance and faith without the preceding work of God in regeneration. It is easy, therefore, to see that conversion is the fruit of all these things. In conversion we are turned round so that whereas once we ran from God, now all is different and our desires are toward Him. We have "put off" (Ephesians 4: 22) the old ways of life and now follow after righteousness. It is now true of us, as Peter said of those to whom he wrote, "The time past of our life may suffice us to have wrought the will of the Gentiles" (1 Peter 4: 3). "God be thanked," says Paul, "that ye were the servants of sin, but ye have obeyed from the heart that form of doctrine which was delivered you" (Romans 6: 17).

Some people talk about a "second" conversion. By this they mean that after having been brought to know the Lord on the first occasion, they had wandered away from Him into paths of sin and foolishness, but by God's grace they have been turned back again to Him. This "second" conversion does not mean that they are a second time regenerated. This is impossible. It merely means that because of the life of God in their soul they find themselves longing for Him once more.

NOT ALL EXPERIENCES OF CONVERSION ARE ALIKE
Although there are these essential things belonging to true conversion, and although these features must be found in everybody who claims to have been converted, we must not make the mistake of thinking that every experience is of the same type.

The Bible helps us here. Saul of Tarsus was converted by a very sudden experience which was the culmination of a long process in which he had been resisting the voice of conscience (Acts 9: 1-6). The jailor at Philippi seems to have been converted through the overwhelming conviction that came upon him of his need in the midst of the earthquake which shook the prison (Acts 16: 25-34). The case was very different, however, with two others of whom the New Testament tells us. There was a woman named Lydia, and we are told about her that she was one "whose heart the Lord opened, that she attended unto the things which were spoken of Paul" (Acts 16: 14). This would seem to have been like the gentle opening of a bud under the influence of the warm sunshine. Timothy appears to have been brought to know God when he was but a boy. He knew the Scriptures "from a child" (2 Timothy 3: 15), probably having been taught them by his grandmother and his mother (2 Timothy 1: 5).

Do not compare your experience with that of someone else, therefore, but check yourself by the Bible. Do you show the marks of one who has truly experienced a "Right About Turn"?

CHAPTER 8

One of the first acts in conversion is faith, and I think of it as

STRETCHING OUT TWO HANDS

It is an old story, but beautiful still. The city of Pompeii had been buried beneath the great volcanic eruption which had destroyed it. When these ruins were being excavated many years afterwards, the pathetic form of a little child was found, with two hands stretched out in mute appeal to the mother who was vainly endeavouring to reach the spot in time to rescue the little one. How eloquent are those two outstretched hands!

FAITH

It is with something of these thoughts as the background of our study that I want to think about faith in this chapter. Faith is "stretching out two hands". There is a striking verse in the Bible which reads, "Ethiopia shall soon stretch out her hands unto God" (Psalm 68: 31). There can be no better or more vivid picture of faith than this.

FAITH EXPRESSES NEED

The man who trusts in God is making the acknowledgment that he is insufficient of himself. Faith is the empty hand stretched out in the humble admission of poverty.

> Nothing in my hand I bring,
> Simply to Thy Cross I cling.

57

So wrote Toplady. Spurgeon used so often to quote these lines in his sermons and prayers that a critic wrote an open letter to the press telling him that his congregation was sufficiently informed of the vacuity of his hand. To this the quick-witted preacher replied that he had to speak to God like this for it was *always* true, "Nothing in my hand I bring".

Real faith is empty-handed. So long as we cling to some proud or secret thought of doing something for ourselves, so long as we try to hold some sin, or tenaciously cling to some brave resolution by which we hope to "work our passage", we do not truly come to God in faith.

Faith is based on repentance; and repentance means that we have come to a complete change of mind about ourselves, that we have given up all confidence in our own righteousness and are now looking to God for mercy and pardon.

OUR PRIDE GETS IN THE WAY

How slow we are to come to God in this "empty-handed" way. We are often like the Jewish people of Paul's day of whom he wrote, "I bear them record that they have a zeal of God, but not according to knowledge. For they being ignorant of God's righteousness, and going about to establish their own righteousness, have not submitted themselves unto the righteousness of God" (Romans 10: 2, 3).

WHAT PAUL REALISED

The position to which Paul himself had been brought is described clearly by him in his letter to the Philippians, chapter 3. He says in this that he now belongs to those who "have no confidence in the flesh" (verse 3). By this phrase he means that he no longer relies on his own independent good deeds, not even his best "religious" ones. (Whenever Paul uses the word "flesh" in places like this, it stands for what a man is apart from the life of the Holy Spirit within him.) In this same chapter Paul says that if anybody could be thought of as having good grounds for boasting, he was one of them. Was he not the most religious of all the Jews? Yes, he was, but, says he, "what things were gain to me, those I counted loss for Christ. Yea doubtless, and I count all things but loss for the excellency of the knowledge of Christ Jesus my Lord: for whom I have suffered the loss of all things, and do count them but dung, that I may win Christ, and be found in him, not having mine own righteousness, which is of the law, but that which is through the faith of Christ, the righteousness which is of God by faith" (Philippians 3: 7-9).

This empty-handedness of faith is further explained when our Lord says in the "Beatitudes" of Matthew, chapter 5: "Blessed are the poor in spirit: for theirs is the kingdom of heaven" (verse 3).

Faith is humble. Some are too proud to ask and to receive. They want to pay: they want to do "some great thing". (Read the interesting story of Naaman at this point. You will find it in 2 Kings 5: 1-14, and note especially verses 11 and 13.) Faith is at the farthest distance from the spirit of pride: it simply asks with outstretched empty hands of need.

FAITH IS READY TO TAKE

A man once knocked at my door and said he was hungry and without a bed for the night. Having an arrangement with a nearby hostel for men, I wrote out a note for him which would procure him both food and bed if he were to present it to the superintendent of the hostel. The man declined to accept my gift. Of course, he was not in need and had been "telling the tale".

Faith that knows its need always takes: this is because the need is so real and so urgent. Faith is the hand that reaches forward to receive. This same action of "taking" or "receiving" has similarly been illustrated by our Lord in the picture of eating and drinking. It is to faith that our Lord is referring when He says in John 6, "I am the living

59

bread which came down from heaven: if any man eat of this bread, he shall live for ever" (verse 51). He went on to say, "Verily, verily, I say unto you, Except ye eat the flesh of the Son of man, and drink his blood, ye have no life in you. Whoso eateth my flesh, and drinketh my blood, hath eternal life; and I will raise him up at the last day. For my flesh is meat indeed, and my blood is drink indeed. He that eateth my flesh, and drinketh my blood, dwelleth in me, and I in him" (verses 53-56).

The same pictorial way of speaking of faith appears again in the book of Revelation. In chapter 22, verse 17, "Let him that is athirst come. And whosoever will, let him take the water of life freely". Note the words carefully—"let him take". That is what faith does. "What shall I render unto the Lord for all his benefits toward me?" asks the Psalmist. He replied, "I will take the cup of salvation, and call upon the name of the Lord" (Psalm 116: 12-13).

FAITH IS MORE THAN AGREEING WITH AN IDEA

By now you will have clearly seen that faith is more than mental assent. It is more than remarking, "O yes, I believe that is true". It is more than mere belief, for "the devils also believe, and tremble" (James 2: 19). Faith is a personal trust: it is the real and earnest committal of yourself to Christ the Saviour. John Calvin once said, "Faith is not a distant view, but a warm embrace of Christ".

> Think not the faith by which the just shall live
> Is a dead creed, a map correct of heaven,
> Far less a feeling fond and fugitive,
> A thoughtless gift, withdrawn as soon as given;
> It is an affirmation and an act
> Which makes eternal truth be present fact!
> (H. Coleridge)

THE STRONG REALITIES OF FAITH

We all know the yarn about a school-boy who defined faith as "believing wot ain't". It is nothing of the kind, of course. Faith is the assurance of things hoped for, the proving of things not seen (Hebrews 11: 1, R.V.). The committing of one's self to God in the act of personal faith means the experiencing of "proving" the reality of God's promises. There is "venture" in faith, but too many of us linger shivering on the brink and fear to launch away. Not long ago in a Lancashire school the following note was received. "Dear Teacher, Please do you mind if David does not go to the baths until he can swim." But how much "faith" is of this kind! Faith takes the plunge and finds that "underneath are the everlasting arms" (Deuteronomy 33: 27).

TRUST

It has been so wisely said that "God is a Father to be trusted —not a problem to be solved". Read Psalm 56 for an incentive to trust God in this way.

> It is God's will that I should cast
> My care on Him each day;
> He also asks me not to cast
> My confidence away.
>
> But O! how foolishly I act
> When taken unawares!
> I cast away my confidence
> And carry all my cares!

FAITH COMMITS US TO A PERSON

Faith of this kind is directed towards a Person, and that Person is the Lord Jesus Christ. Faith, therefore, has about it all those warm and intimate things that belong to the relation between two persons. The real believer—the man of faith—knows the Lord Himself. He speaks to Him in prayer and listens to His voice by the reading of the Bible. The promises and commands of Christ are received as the counsels of One who is loved and known and trusted.

Faith is never without knowledge, but it must not be confused with it. A true believer may perhaps know very little about this or about that, but he knows the One whom he is trusting.

FAITH IN GOD'S PROMISES

We have already begun to see that faith fastens on a word. It believes the promises and takes them to heart. This is where the Bible provides such food for faith. We are given exceeding great and precious promises (2 Peter 1: 4), and faith takes hold of these. How clearly this is exemplified in the life of Abraham who, we are told, "staggered not at the promise of God through unbelief; but was strong in faith, giving glory to God; and being fully persuaded that, what he had promised, he was able also to perform" (Romans 4: 20-21). A man once came to Jesus about his boy. "Sir," he said, "come down ere my child die." To this Jesus replied, "Go thy way; thy son liveth." And the man believed the word that Jesus had spoken to him, and he went his way (John 4: 49-50). That was faith.

GOD ALWAYS HONOURS FAITH

When we stretch out our hands to God, will it be in vain? No. The Saviour said, "Him that cometh to me I will in no wise cast out" (John 6: 37). In this He was but endorsing the words of the prophet in Isaiah 55: 1-2: "Ho, every one that thirsteth, come ye to the waters, and he that hath no money; come ye, buy, and eat; yea, come, buy wine and milk without money and without price. Wherefore do ye spend money for that which is not bread? and your labour for that which satisfieth not? Hearken diligently unto me, and eat ye that which is good, and let your soul delight itself in fatness." The truth is summed up in the great words of Romans 6: 23: "The gift of God is eternal life through Jesus Christ our Lord."

Come to God and ask. Bring your needs; pray out of your feelings; let your requests be made known to God. Stretch out your hands to Him, for nobody ever seeks in vain.

CHAPTER 9

In this chapter we look at one of the results of our faith. I call it

A NEW STANDING GROUND

Have you ever been with someone who is trying to defend himself, and he is putting up such a lame excuse and giving such a poor explanation that you have had to tell him that he has not a leg to stand on? You know what this means. It means that he cannot excuse himself or give any satisfactory explanation of the conduct which is being called in question.

NO EXCUSE

This is our position before God. Paul makes it plain to us that all the world is guilty before Him, and every mouth is stopped. See what he says in Romans 3: 19-20: "Now we know that what things soever the law saith, it saith to them who are under the law: that every mouth may be stopped, and all the world may become guilty before God. Therefore by the deeds of the law there shall no flesh be justified in his sight: for by the law is the knowledge of sin." Nobody has any "excuse" (Romans 1: 20).

All this means that in the presence of God we have no standing. We are guilty, and are therefore condemned. One of the chief things lost by us through our sin was our acceptance with God.

63

It is with this problem of our standing with God that the word "justification" has to do. What does it mean? Look at the following verses.

Exodus 23: 7, "Keep thee far from a false matter; and the innocent and righteous slay thou not: for I will not justify the wicked".

Deuteronomy 25: 1, "If there be a controversy between men, and they come unto judgment, that the judges may judge them; then they shall justify the righteous, and condemn the wicked".

Proverbs 17: 15, "He that justifieth the wicked, and he that condemneth the just, even they both are abomination to the Lord".

Luke 16: 15, "And he said unto them, Ye are they which justify yourselves before men; but God knoweth your hearts: for that which is highly esteemed among men is abomination in the sight of God".

Romans 2: 13, "For not the hearers of the law are just before God, but the doers of the law shall be justified".

An examination of these passages shows that the word has to do with the verdict of a judge. Strictly speaking, it does not primarily refer to the kind of person or character that a man is, but rather to his relation to the law.

THE CLAIMS OF VIOLATED LAW

The law has a claim against a man if he has violated it in some way. If the law has no such claim against a man he is declared "just", that is to say, he is "justified". Justification relates to a man's standing in the eyes of the law, and, in some respects, the sort of character he has comes into consideration only in a remote and secondary way. If a man breaks the law he becomes liable to its penalty, and so the legal verdict is that he is condemned. Should he pay the fine or endure the imprisonment he has completely met the claims of the law, even though in character he may still be a bad and unworthy person. The law, however, has no claims upon him, in the way of penalties: that means he is a "justified" man.

HOW CAN A SINNER BE JUSTIFIED?

Let us now apply all this to our relation to God's holy Law. As we have seen, "All have sinned, and come short of the glory of God" (Romans 3: 23). We are under the penalties of the broken Law. How can the situation be handled? Can it be managed by a strenuous effort on our own part to "turn over a new leaf"? Can we meet the difficulty by resolving to keep God's Law? Hear the answer from the Bible itself. It is found in the words of Romans 3: 20: "Therefore by the deeds of the law there shall no flesh be justified in his sight: for by the law is the knowledge of sin." Galatians 2: 16, reads, "Knowing that a man is not justified by the works of the law, but by the faith of Jesus Christ, even we have believed in Jesus Christ, that we might be justified by the faith of Christ, and not by the works of the law: for by the works of the law shall no flesh be justified".

The Bible is thus very plain in its teaching that we cannot obtain justification by "the works of the law".

JUSTIFICATION IS GOD'S GIFT

If we cannot earn a new standing before God, we must receive it in some other way. This way, the Bible says, is by a "gift". Go back again to Romans chapter 3, but this time read verse 24: "Being justified freely by his grace through the redemption that is in Christ Jesus." This gift has to be received, and the way we receive it is by "faith". This is made clear in Romans 3: 26, "To declare, I say, at this time his righteousness: that he might be just, and the justifier of him which believeth in Jesus". Romans 5: 1, says the same thing, "Therefore being justified by faith, we have peace with God through our Lord Jesus Christ".

OUR NEW STANDING GROUND IS IN CHRIST

Look again at these two verses. They both direct our

faith to the Lord Jesus Christ. Quite correct! It is the work that Christ has done that provides the ground on which the sinner can be declared "free from the law". Romans 5: 9 speaks of us "being now justified by (or 'in', R.V. margin) his blood". The word "blood" here stands for the death of Christ. Turn now to Galatians 3: 13, and read it carefully. Having done this, look now at the following verse: "For he hath made him to be sin for us, who knew no sin; that we might be made the righteousness of God in him" (2 Corinthians 5: 21).

OUR LORD'S SAVING WORK

The work of Christ in saving us gives us a new standing ground. By reason of what He has done in taking our guilt upon Himself, meeting the requirements of the broken Law, and bearing its penalties in His own heart, He has secured for us a new position in relation to that Law. Apart from Christ we stand before the Judge of all the earth condemned as a prisoner in the dock. What our Saviour did was to put Himself in our place. (Refresh your memory in Chapter Five.) We have already seen that when a fine is paid, or an imprisonment is undergone, the person concerned is completely discharged from the claims of the law that he has broken. He has met those claims in the form of penalty. For the sinner this has been done by Christ, and the benefits of Christ's work in this way are summed up in the New Testament by the word "justification".

A DEFINITION

Let us try to define to ourselves what we mean by this great word in our Christian faith. So far as the relations of God and the sinner are concerned, justification may be regarded as "a judicial act of God, in which He declares, on the basis of the righteousness of Jesus Christ, that all the claims of the law are satisfied with respect to the sinner". In 1 Corinthians 6 Paul has been describing the sins of the great and evil city of Corinth and then says, "And such were some of you: but ye are washed, but ye are sanctified, but ye are justified in the name of the Lord Jesus, and by the Spirit of our God" (verse 11). This means that we have a new standing ground. All the condemnation is gone, and there is absolutely nothing against us any more. See Acts 13: 39, Romans 8: 1, 33, and 34, and Philippians 3: 9.

JUSTIFICATION IS "ONCE-FOR-ALL"

Our justification admits us into the privileges of restored relations with God. Justification is more than forgiveness, for we may be forgiven—by God's goodness—again and again. We may find forgiveness as often as we need it and seek it. Justification is a kind of once-for-all act by which God has been pleased to receive us in the merits of the Saviour. This is the strong ground under our feet which cannot be shaken. As sinners saved by God's grace, you and I may not presume upon this and continue in sin. "God forbid," says Paul in Romans 6: 2. But we may be assured that however much we stumble and fall through our weakness our position in Christ is secure.

> My hope is built on nothing less
> Than Jesus' blood and righteousness;
> I dare not trust the sweetest frame
> But wholly lean on Jesus' Name.
>
> On Christ, the solid Rock I stand;
> All other ground is sinking sand.

Do you stand here?

CHAPTER 10

*Our last chapter finished with Paul's horrified, "God forbid!",
when the suggestion of continuing in sin was mentioned. But, we
may ask*

IS IT POSSIBLE NOT TO SIN?

We have already made some attempt to understand what
the Bible teaches about sin, but just now we are thinking
about our actions of "sinning". Is it possible not to do this?
Here is a practical question to which we must find an
answer, otherwise our Christian life seems a disappointment.
Let us find our answer by making this lesson something of
a straightforward Bible study. I want you to have your
Bible with you and turn to each passage and look at it and
think it over with me.

WHERE SIN COMES FROM

Suppose we start with the words in James 1: 13-15: "Let
no man say when he is tempted, I am tempted of God: for
God cannot be tempted with evil, neither tempteth he any
man: but every man is tempted, when he is drawn away of
his own lust, and enticed. Then when lust hath conceived,
it bringeth forth sin: and sin, when it is finished, bringeth
forth death."

These words make it clear that the enticements to evil
do not come from God. They come from our own hearts.
When we have given way to such inner enticements to evil
then we have committed sin.

THE FIRST SIN

Go back now to Genesis 3:6. "And when the woman saw that the tree was good for food, and that it was pleasant to the eyes, and a tree to be desired to make one wise, she took of the fruit thereof, and did eat, and gave also unto her husband with her; and he did eat." This verse indicates that what James has described is exactly what occurred in the first sin. The action came entirely from the woman's own thoughts and desires. It is true, those thoughts and desires had been instilled into her mind by the tempter, but they became properly her own when she accepted them.

THE STATE OF MAN'S HEART

The habit of sinning is now fixed in us all. Turn to Genesis 8:21, where you find the words: "For the imagination of man's heart is evil from his youth." David confesses this same thing in Psalm 51:5: "Behold, I was shapen in iniquity; and in sin did my mother conceive me."

Even the best of men, in their highest and holiest moments, have had to confess that sin mars all that they do. Look at the words of Isaiah 6:5: "Then said I, Woe is me! for I am undone; because I am a man of unclean lips, and I dwell in the midst of a people of unclean lips: for mine eyes have seen the King, the Lord of hosts." In Job 42:6, he says, "I abhor myself, and repent in dust and ashes". In Ezra 9:6, "O my God, I am ashamed and blush to lift up my face to thee, my God: for our iniquities are increased over our head, and our trespass is grown up unto the heavens". Even the man of God, John, confesses in 1 John 1:8: "If we say that we have no sin, we deceive ourselves, and the truth is not in us."

Turn now in your Bible to Romans 7 and make a very careful note of the words in verses 14 to 19. This is the perplexing situation in which we find ourselves. It is no wonder that we find our hearts concurring with Paul when he exclaimed, "O wretched man that I am! Who shall deliver me from the body of this death?" (verse 24).

ONE WHO NEVER SINNED

This last verse that we have quoted turns our minds in a brighter direction, and we may now change the subject a little. Into this race of sinful and sinning men and women there came One who never sinned. The Lord Jesus Christ, God's only Son, living a truly human life, was "without sin". Turn to 1 Peter 2: 22. "Who did no sin, neither was guile found in his mouth." Observe the description which Peter gives of the Lord in his sermon recorded in Acts 3: 14. "The holy One and the Just." Turning to Paul we find clear words in 2 Corinthians 5: 21: "Who knew no sin," and John in 1 John 3: 5 writes: "And ye know that he was manifested to take away our sins; and in him is no sin". He has previously described the Lord in 1 John 2: 1 as "Jesus Christ the righteous". The epistle to the Hebrews records in chapter 4, verse 15 that He was "in all points tempted like as we are, yet without sin". Again, in Hebrews 7: 26, He is described as "holy, harmless, undefiled, separate from sinners".

We do well at this point also to notice our Lord's own testimony concerning Himself. In John 8: 29, He said, "I do always those things that please him", and in John 8: 46, we find He was able to face His critics with the question, "Which of you convinceth me of sin?" So far as the temptations of Satan are concerned, Jesus was able to say of Himself in John 14: 30: "The prince of this world cometh, and hath nothing in me". This last expression means that when the devil approached the Lord there was no subtle traitor within His heart to whom the evil seductions of the tempter could make appeal. In endorsement of all these things there stands written the word which God the Father spoke from heaven, recorded in Matthew 3: 17: "This is my beloved Son, in whom I am well pleased."

What is the meaning of all this? It means that there came into a race of sinning persons One who never sinned, and that He came in order that the power of sin might be broken in us, so that we, too, might find it "possible not to sin".

Let us go back to our Bibles again, and in the opening chapter of Matthew, verse 21, we find the words, "Thou shalt call his name JESUS: for he shall save his people from their sins". Someone has rightly said that this does not read, He shall save His people "in their sins". The purpose of our Lord's salvation was to deliver us from the guilt of our past sin, and at this present moment to save us from the power of sin, and in the glorious future to free us from the very presence of it. Turn over to the Fourth Gospel, and in John 5: 14 you will find that our Lord said to the man whom He had healed, "Sin no more". This is exactly what He said also to the woman found guilty of adultery in John 8: 11. "Neither do I condemn thee: go, and sin no more."

WE MUST NOT SIN

It is unthinkable that those who know the forgiveness of sins should live any longer in the habit of them. The purpose of our salvation is that we should no longer sin. We are not surprised therefore to observe the consternation of Paul at this thought in Romans 6. The whole of this chapter ought to be carefully studied. Look at verse 6, with its words: "That henceforth we should not serve sin." In verses 11-13: "Reckon ye also yourselves to be dead indeed unto sin. . . . Let not sin therefore reign in your mortal body, that ye should obey it in the lusts thereof. Neither yield ye your members as instruments of unrighteousness unto sin." At verse 14 we discover a great and invigorating statement: "For sin shall not have dominion over you." Verse 18 reminds us that we have been "made free from sin", and you will find these same words in verse 22. Read carefully the practical words of Ephesians 4: 25-32. In 1 John 2: 1 the apostle writes: "My little children, these things write I unto you, that ye sin not."

IF A CHRISTIAN SINS

John does not mean that no Christian ever sins, for he has already said that if we say that we have no sin we deceive ourselves, and he immediately follows on these words in chapter 2 by saying that "if any man sin, we have an advocate with the Father, Jesus Christ the righteous". He does make it plain, however, that the Christian must not sin, and need not sin. It is quite inconsistent with the Christian life that anyone should keep on in the habit and practice of sinning. It is this idea of the habit and practice of sinning that is in John's mind when he says that the true believer "cannot sin" (1 John 3: 9), that is, cannot go on living in sin.

We have now been able to see, first of all, how strong the grip of sin is on our lives, and also that there appeared among us One in whom sin was not found, and that because of this those who follow Him are urged not to sin. How does this all come to effect? Turn over to Jude, verse 24, and let the words burn themselves into your heart: "Him that is able to keep you from falling." Do you believe this? If so, you are believing the Gospel itself. In Romans 8: 2 Paul explains that it is through the power of Christ's, indwelling life in us by the Holy Spirit that we are made victorious.

OVERCOMERS

There can be no doubt at all that we are intended by our Saviour to be overcomers. Look up the words in Revelation 2: 7, 11, 17, 26 and 3: 5, 12 and 21. In Revelation 12: 11 it has been written, "And they overcame him by the blood of the Lamb". This last reference is an important one. It is only through our Lord's victory at the Cross that we may have any victory in our day by day experience.

73

Is it possible not to sin? Let us finish with two more quotations. "I can do all things through Christ which strengtheneth me" (Philippians 4: 13). "In all these things we are more than conquerors through him that loved us" (Romans 8: 37).

CHAPTER 11

Perseverance is to be the feature of the Christian life, but

HOW DO I KEEP GOING?

"That thing won't go." This was the comment of an old countryman the first time he saw a stationary railway locomotive. "That thing won't stop" was the exclamation he uttered when later he saw one hurtling along the rails. The question of starting and stopping belongs to almost every aspect of experience, not the least being the Christian experience.

"I am afraid to start," says an honest man who has proved to himself by painful experiences what a hopeless person he is at fulfilling his own resolves. "I'm afraid to start, because I don't think I could keep it up." This is the problem—keeping it up. How, then, is the Christian life maintained?

It is maintained because it is *life*, and so goes on the same way as all life goes on. The elementary things of nourishment, air, and exercise which, being translated into terms of Christian experience, are Bible reading, prayer and Christian service, are taken for granted. No one can continue the Christian life without paying attention to these things. But this is not all. The fact is that it is not ultimately your life or mine that is in question. It is the life of another: it is the life of Christ.

75

The Bible makes it perfectly plain that Christ is our life. A famous sentence from the New Testament, but one which ought to be known better, is the one that Paul uses about his own Christian life. The passage is often referred to as "Galatians Two Twenty". There is an immense amount of truth in this verse, and it has a lot to say about the way the Christian life can be maintained.

"I am crucified with Christ: nevertheless I live; yet not I, but Christ liveth in me: and the life which I now live in the flesh I live by the faith of the Son of God, who loved me, and gave himself for me." This verse means that when Christ died *we* were accounted to have died also, and in this way we may regard ourselves as on the resurrection side of death and so now "alive unto God" (Romans 6: 11). All this is experienced by faith in Christ. It is as we trust in Christ that He lives in us. But more about this as we go along.

CHRISTIAN LIFE IS NOT A NEW RESOLUTION

This is one of the points Paul discusses in Romans, chapter 7. If you look at this chapter, especially verses 14 onwards, you will see how futile is the endeavour to seek sanctification by means of "the law". (Sanctification, of course, is the New Testament word for the kind of life that a healthy Christian lives: we shall examine this word in more detail in another chapter.) Romans 7 is one of the "big" passages of the Bible. It comes in the context of a previous discussion in which Paul has demonstrated, firstly, that by the Law is the knowledge of sin, that is, the Law can now do nothing but condemn us. Secondly, Paul has shown that nobody can secure a right standing with God on the merits of what they have done in the way of good works. The apostle's point in chapter 7 is to show that, similarly, no man can be "sanctified" by "works of the law". The reason for this is to be found in the extremely broken condition of man's moral life.

Look at what Paul says in verses 15 and 16. The Authorised Version (A.V.) words read, "For that which I do I allow not: for what I would, that do I not; but what I hate, that do I. If then I do that which I would not, I consent unto the law that it is good". Paraphrasing this, and bringing out the force of some of Paul's specially chosen words, we may put it this way: "The effects that follow from my actions are just the very things that I cannot sanction. Somehow I do not practise the things that my conscience approves. It is clear, therefore, that if I perform things which my conscience disapproves, I am at the same time giving judgment that what the Law requires is perfectly right." Paul continues a little later in verse 21 by saying, "There is a law of behaviour that governs my actions, for when I want to do what is right I discover a tendency to evil that hinders me".

Brave resolutions—praiseworthy in themselves—do not constitute the Christian life. We are unable to do those very things we resolve to do, and this is because sin has unfitted us to do so.

But secondly,

CHRISTIAN LIFE IS NOT KEEPING NEW RULES

We need some balanced thinking here, for the Christian must not "snap his fingers" at the holy Law of God. The Christian is certainly no longer "under" the Law as a means of right standing or acceptance with God; nor is the Christian sensible when he tries to use the Law as an instrument of Christian living: but, at the same time, the Christian is not out of all relation to Law. Though Law-keeping is not a successful *means* of holiness of life, it is, nevertheless, true that a holy life is a real *fulfilment* of the righteous requirements of the Law. This is stated clearly in Romans 8: 4, where Paul affirms that the purpose of God's saving grace is "that the righteousness (that is, the righteous requirements) of the law might be fulfilled in us".

In our last section we discussed the Law first of all in the light of our resolve to keep it and then in the light of the corruption of fallen human nature which cannot keep it. What we are now specially looking at is the whole idea of "rule-keeping" as such. Again, in a later chapter we are going into the question of Christian conduct—"Should a Christian . . .?" But just now let us be clear that we are not under a new list of "Do's and Don'ts".

I expect you have wished already that there was some set of "rules" for you. When I was a very young believer I was much helped by being given a little decorated card which was headed "Six Short Rules for Young Christians". This was truly useful in its own way and gave me the necessary guidance in simple things, but it was in no sense a code of Christian behaviour. There is no set of rules. Rule-keeping is bondage, but we have been called into freedom. This freedom, of course, is consistent with genuine obedience to the Law of God, but it is much more than merely working to rules.

CHRISTIAN LIFE IS NOT KEEPING UP A NEW APPEARANCE

There are just a few very simple but quite straightforward things that have to be said under this heading.

"Appearances are deceptive"—so the saying runs, and how true this can be with religion. It is often thought that Christian life is to be equated with wearing a black coat and a white collar, or with a special "suit for Sundays", or having a "holy tone for Sundays". There is a terrible danger of putting on a show of outward conformity to the conventional ways of church-going, hymn singing and Bible reading. A man may get a full attack of "meeting-itis", but this is not the Christian life. "This people honoureth me with their lips, but their heart is far from me" (Mark 7: 6). God used these words of some people long ago who kept up a very fine appearance.

Do not make a mistake. The Christian life will give you a new appearance in every way, but it will be more than skin deep. We are to live a distinctive life, but the emphasis is to be placed not on distinctive "oddities" or on a slavish

conformity to the "done thing"; the emphasis is on "life".
For this we turn to our next paragraph.

CHRISTIAN LIFE IS "LIFE"

Two small boys whom I knew some time ago went to
stay in the country with their grandfather. At the side
of the house was a fruit tree which that season had yielded
no fruit. In grandfather's absence one day the boys hatched
a "clever plot" to play a trick on grandfather. Collecting
some apples from a bowl, and procuring some black
thread, they proceeded to tie a number of apples skilfully
on the branches of the tree. Eagerly they awaited grandfather's return and then invited him to accompany them
into the garden and to witness the fact that there were
apples on the tree after all! Grandfather came out and,
after being duly impressed, quietly remarked to the boys.
"Well, that's the first time I've seen apples grow on that
pear tree".

All this is a parable. It is poor work tying fruit on dead
branches: it is similarly poor work trying to "add" Christian virtues to a dead character. The only way to produce
fruit is to grow it: the only way to produce spiritual goodness is likewise to grow it. It is the result of life. If there is
the right kind of life there will be the right kind of fruit.
Our Lord said, "Every good tree bringeth forth good fruit;
but a corrupt tree bringeth forth evil fruit. A good tree
cannot bring forth evil fruit, neither can a corrupt tree
bring forth good fruit. . . . Wherefore by their fruits ye
shall know them" (Matthew 7: 17, 18, 20).

Life is natural, spontaneous, effortless. Is there this spon-
taneity about your Christian life? Remember, Christianity
is "life".

But we must say a little more.

CHRISTIAN LIFE IS "NEW" LIFE

In one sense, our old way of going on before we were
converted and before our consciences were made sensitive

to God was a kind of spontaneous life. We did whatever occurred to us just because we wanted to, and we thought no more about it. If we wanted to be rude to someone, we were; if we felt it was necessary to tell a lie to get out of an awkward corner, we did; if we wanted to indulge in some lust, we did. Yes! All was natural and gay. But was it? Our Lord spoke of a "corrupt tree", and the principles of fruit production on a corrupt tree are much the same as those with a "good" tree. But this, of course, does not conclude the matter. First "make the tree good", said our Lord. Once this has been done, the tree can be relied upon to bear good fruit. It is like this in the Christian life: it is "new" life. Do you remember what "Galatians Two Twenty" says? It is "Christ liveth in me".

When I was a young believer a preacher visited the church to which I belonged, and startled the congregation by saying, "A Christian does as he likes!" All sat up to take notice, and then he quietly added, *"for he has a new set of likes"*. Yes! The tree has been made good. So long as the "new" life is abundant and active, the behaviour can take care of itself.

The climax of all this is that

CHRISTIAN LIFE IS CHRIST'S LIFE

From the moment you were born again and converted, and throughout all the chapters of this book so far, you have been realising that *everything is in the Lord Jesus Christ*. He is all, and without Him we have nothing whatever. This is particularly true in the question of Christian life about which we are now thinking.

The standard to which we seek to bring our lives is that of Christlikeness (more about this later). But you may be tempted to ask, how can "Christ" be seen in us? Let me ask you another question in return. How can you see "me" in me? It is because it is I who am standing before you. Now let us repeat the first question. How can "Christ" be seen in us? It is because it is HE who is in us. Let us go back again to "Galatians Two Twenty". Here Paul says, "Christ liveth in me". He does this by His Holy Spirit, as Paul points out in Romans 8: 9 and 10, and elsewhere.

Let another illustration conclude this chapter. The on-looker at a game of football always sees most of the game, and, if he is enthusiastic, tries to put something of himself into the players whom he is supporting. Imagine you are such a spectator. You are feeling—"if only I could get 'inside' the man!" You are sure then that he would do the thing you think to be right. Lift this now to the highest level. Our Lord is no mere onlooker, but a participator in our struggles. He does not merely cheer us from a distant grand stand, but puts Himself within us, enabling us to do and to be all that He wills. Our Lord has definitely taken up His abode *within* us, and this happened at our conversion. In so far as we are trustful and obedient to Him, He will live out His Divine life through our human experience. "Christ in you, the hope of glory" (Colossians 1: 27)—and, we may add, the hope of "keeping going" too.

CHAPTER 12

Talking about "Keeping going" brings us right up against

THE STANDARDS TO BE REACHED

In the Christian life everything is new. I expect you have learned to sing the hymn which has the verse in it:

> Heaven above is softer blue,
>   Earth around is sweeter green;
> Something lives in every hue
>   Christless eyes have never seen:
> Birds with gladder songs o'erflow,
>   Flowers with deeper beauties shine,
> Since I know, as now I know,
>   I am His, and He is mine.

Paul put this experience strikingly for us in the words of 2 Corinthians 5: 17: "Therefore if any man be in Christ, he is a new creature; old things are passed away; behold, all things are become new." This "newness of life" (Romans 6: 4) is outwardly expressed by living according to new standards. The Christian may not go on as he always did. His life must be different. John the Baptist urged those who came to him professing repentance to perform works "meet for repentance" (Matthew 3: 8).

Old things are most certainly to pass right away. There are some things that are to be left behind. Read very carefully and slowly the words which Paul writes in Ephesians 4: 22-32. Here is a list of some of the things that are to go. We are to put away lying; and we are to cease from sinful anger; "let him that stole, steal no more"; we are to be finished with unclean speech; bitterness, wrath, anger, clamour, evil speaking and malice are to be put away.

There is a terrible list of things which Paul calls "the works of the flesh" in Galatians 5: 19-21, and he concludes this list by saying, "that they which do such things shall not inherit the kingdom of God". Writing to the Romans he summarises this aspect of our Christian experience by saying, "Let us therefore cast off the works of darkness, and let us put on the armour of light" (Romans 13: 12). These are some of the important teachings that we began to learn when we were studying the nature of conversion. Refresh your mind on that.

THERE ARE NEW STANDARDS

Are there new standards? Yes, there are! One writer has said that there is a kind of deadly delusion abroad, in which it appears to be thought that there are two standards of Christian character and conduct, and that each believer is free to say under which he will place himself—the higher or the lower. If he is charged with unchristian action or temper, he replies, "O, but, you know, I do not profess ...". What does he not profess? Men of the world know that he professes to be a follower of Christ, and this is enough. There is only one standard for the Christian, and that is the highest. There are new standards for the Christian, and these make up what we commonly call Christian behaviour.

SANCTIFICATION

The word that is most often found in the New Testament

for these new standards as expressed in life is the word "sanctification" or "holiness". These two English words both represent the same Greek word. Sanctification, which really means a purity of heart and mind and action which is consistent with the idea of one who has been set apart for God, is God's standard for us. In 1 Thessalonains 5: 22 and 23, we have these words, "Abstain from all appearance of evil. And the very God of peace sanctify you wholly; and I pray God your whole spirit and soul and body be preserved blameless unto the coming of our Lord Jesus Christ". In the previous chapter at verse 3 Paul says, "this is the will of God, even your sanctification".

Our Lord Himself taught this in the Sermon on the Mount. He says, "Ye have heard that it hath been said, Thou shalt love thy neighbour, and hate thine enemy. But I say unto you, Love your enemies, bless them that curse you, do good to them that hate you, and pray for them which despitefully use you, and persecute you. . . . Be ye therefore perfect, even as your Father which is in heaven is perfect" (Matthew 5: 43, 44, 48). Here are new standards indeed! Sanctification is not like taking a journey without knowing where we are going. The path is plotted and mapped for us.

CHRIST IS THE PATTERN

It would be true to say that the standards to be reached are set before us very plainly in the Lord Jesus Himself. He is the pattern, and likeness to Christ is what we are to seek. He embodies the new standards that we are to reach. In 1 Peter 2: 21, we have the following words: "For even here-unto were ye called: because Christ also suffered for us, leaving us an example, that ye should follow his steps." Paul had spoken similarly in Philippians 2: 5: "Let this mind be in you, which was also in Christ Jesus;" and John in 1 John 2: 6, says, "He that saith he abideth in him ought himself also so to walk, even as he walked".

THE EXAMPLE GIVEN IN THE UPPER ROOM

This truth had been very forcibly and vividly pressed home to the consciences of the disciples by our Lord in His action in the Upper Room. John 13 records the story of our Lord having washed the feet of the disciples. He did this because the disciples seem to have been too proud to do it for one another. When He finished this menial task and was sat down again, He said to them, "Know ye what I have done to you? Ye call me Master and Lord: and ye say well; for so I am. If I then, your Lord and Master, have washed your feet; ye also ought to wash one another's feet. For I have given you an example, that ye should do as I have done to you. Verily, verily, I say unto you, The servant is not greater than his lord; neither he that is sent greater than he that sent him. If ye know these things, happy are ye if ye do them" (John 13: 12-17).

THE QUALITIES OF CHRISTLIKENESS

The Christian's aim is to grow up to resemble Christ in all things (Ephesians 4: 15); to be conformed to the image of God's Son (Romans 8: 29). The qualities of Christlikeness are seen from a study of our Lord's own character. He was full of tenderness and grace. See how He touched the leper (Mark 1: 41); how He blessed the little children (Mark 10: 13-16); how the common people loved Him (Mark 12: 37; Luke 4: 22; John 7: 46); and how He sympathised with the sorrowing and the needy (Matthew 9: 36; Luke 7: 13; 8: 52; John 11: 33, and 20: 15).

THE MORAL PERFECTION OF JESUS

Our Lord set the standard not only in these ways, but in His moral perfection and sinlessness. It is this exceedingly high standard to which Peter refers in the passage we have already noted, where, having urged us to follow His steps, he goes on to say, "who did no sin, neither was guile found in his mouth: who, when he was reviled, reviled not again" (1 Peter 2: 22, 23). Hebrews 7: 26 describes our

Saviour as "holy, harmless, undefiled, separate from sinners". In 1 John 3: 5, the apostle says of Him, "and in him
is no sin". We can never be exactly as our Lord, because of
the sinful taint that is already within us, but it is gloriously
possible "not to sin", and we have seen this in an earlier
study.

CHRISTIAN VIRTUES

To form a list of Christian virtues would be a very great
task, and the Bible never does this in any extensive manner,
though it is remarkable how wide is the scope of behaviour
and relationships with which the New Testament deals in
this respect. There are instructions for wives and husbands
(Ephesians 5: 22, 25; 1 Peter 3: 7); there is guidance for
parents and for children (Ephesians 6: 4 and 6, and verses 1-
2); there is advice for young men (Titus 2: 6), young
women (Titus 2: 4), aged women (Titus 2: 3), aged men
(Titus 2: 2). Standards are set for those who are masters
(Ephesians 6: 9, and the epistle to Philemon). Guidance is
given to servants (Ephesians 6: 5), and to slaves (1 Peter 2:
18; 1 Timothy 6: 1-2; 1 Corinthians 7: 21). Counsel is
given on citizenship (1 Peter 2: 17; Romans 13: 1), and the
rich are told how they should behave (1 Timothy 6: 17;
James 5: 1-6).

THE FRUIT OF THE NEW LIFE

Every Christian is familiar with the beautiful list of Christian
qualities that Paul gives in Galatians 5: 22, 23: "But the
fruit of the Spirit is love, joy, peace, long-suffering, gentleness, goodness, faith, meekness, temperance (self-control)."
It is profitable to notice as we touch upon this verse that
these lovely qualities are all described as the "fruit" of the
Spirit, that is to say, they are the result of the new life that
salvation has brought. It is in this sense that we are to understand Paul's words in Philippians 2: 12 when he says, "work
out your own salvation with fear and trembling". That
which God has put within is to come out.

Turn to another list of beautiful things in Philippians 4: 8-9. Read the list carefully. Another kind of summary of the Christian standards is given by Paul in his letter to Titus. These latter words are worth studying: "For the grace of God that bringeth salvation hath appeared to all men, teaching us that, denying ungodliness and worldly lusts, we should live soberly, righteously, and godly, in this present world" (Titus 2: 11, 12).

GOOD WORKS

Conformity to these new standards is sometimes called in the New Testament "good works". We must be careful here not to misunderstand the Bible. There are two ways of looking at "good works". The Jews of Paul's day, and unfortunately, many people at the present time, look upon "good works" as something they must strive to do in order to achieve a kind of merit and good standing before God. This is a hopeless undertaking, and all the apostles join together in affirming that we cannot possibly earn our salvation by performing "good works" in this way.

There is another way, however, of thinking of "good works", and the New Testament also presents this to us. "Good works" are the necessary evidence of faith. This is what James pressed for in his epistle in chapter 2. Look, for example, at verse 17: "Faith," he says, "if it hath not works, is dead, being alone." In the next verse he says, "I will show thee my faith by my works". Again in verse 20 he says, "Faith without works is dead". "Good works," then, are the necessary evidence that a man is a true believer. The old commentator on the Bible, Matthew Henry, wrote, "If religion has done nothing for your tempers, it has done nothing for your souls". In Ephesians 2: 10, Paul says, "For we are his workmanship, created in Christ Jesus unto good works, which God hath before ordained that we should walk in them".

88

These "good works" of ours are those by which we are to be tested. 1 Corinthians 3: 13-15 reads, "Every man's work shall be made manifest: for the day shall declare it, because it shall be revealed by fire; and the fire shall try every man's work of what sort it is. If any man's work abide which he hath built thereupon, he shall receive a reward. If any man's work shall be burned, he shall suffer loss: but he himself shall be saved; yet so as by fire". This same truth is expressed in Revelation 22: 12, in which our Lord says that He will "give every man according as his work shall be". For the performing of these good works there is all-sufficient grace. Look up in your Bible the encouraging words of 2 Corinthians 9: 8, and 2 Thessalonians 2: 17.

GOD'S HOLY LAW

The question is sometimes asked, What is the relation of the Christian to the Law of God? The answer is quite plain from one point of view. Paul says in Romans 10: 4, "For Christ is the end of the law for righteousness to every one that believeth". This means that the whole purpose of the Law so far as our justification and standing before God is concerned, has been fulfilled in Christ. There is another aspect of the Law, however, in which it still has authority over us. It is not that by "Law-keeping" we can earn our acceptance with God, but by fulfilling His commandments we are certainly able to show Him that we love Him. This is our Lord's teaching to His disciples. In John 14: 23, "If a man love me, he will keep my words". The Law of God, then, coming to us through the love of God in Christ, constrains us to obedience. This is sometimes called "the obedience of faith" (Romans 16: 26). James has a refreshing word for this and calls it "the royal law" (James 2: 8).

WHY NOT A LIST OF RULES?

As I said in the last chapter, many of us have felt at some time or other that it would be so very good if we could have a list of rules by which to live. In some ways this would be an elementary help, and it is possibly quite good for us in the early weeks and months of our Christian experience to have some "rules" before us. But it is a mistake to think that Christian life can be reduced to rules. We are given the guidance of one great motive for our Christian life, and this determines the standard by which we are to live. Paul says in 1 Corinthians 10: 31, "Whether therefore ye eat, or drink, or whatsoever ye do, do all to the glory of God". In the light of this he tells the Colossians that his great burning passion in all his pastoral ministry is that he "may present every man perfect in Christ Jesus".

These are the standards to be reached.

CHAPTER 13

In this chapter I want you to come to see that because you have been saved by Christ you are His

"PRIVATE PROPERTY"

"What's mine's, my own." Have you ever heard that saying? I expect you have, and more than likely you have said it yourself, either playfully or else in some selfish motive.

"What's mine's, my own;" but is it? Turn to the New Testament and in 1 Corinthians 6: 19-20, we read the following: "What? know ye not that your body is the temple of the Holy Ghost which is in you, which ye have of God, and ye are not your own? For ye are bought with a price: therefore glorify God in your body, and in your spirit, which are God's." Similarly in Romans 14: 7 and 8, it reads: "For none of us liveth to himself, and no man dieth to himself. For whether we live, we live unto the Lord; and whether we die, we die unto the Lord: whether we live therefore, or die, we are the Lord's." The words "Private Property" are to be seen written across every Christian life. This is the meaning of consecration.

DEVOTED TO GOD

In the Old Testament there are many stories of the wars of the Israelites. Battles were fought and won under the leadership of God who was the "Lord of Hosts". When the enemy was routed, the booty left on the battle field was usually collected into a heap. In the normal way, and among other nations, this would have been divided among the soldiery as their legitimate reward. This was not the case, however, with the Israelite victories. The booty was always regarded as belonging to God: it was "devoted". The Bible word that describes this sort of thing in all its wide implications is the word "consecrated". Because it was God's victory, the booty was His. The Israelites accordingly regarded it as dedicated, or "handed over to Him" whose it was.

THE CHRISTIAN BELONGS TO THE REDEEMER

All this is true concerning ourselves. The reason for which we must regard ourselves as the "private property" of the Lord is that we are His as the very spoils of victory. This is the meaning of Isaiah 53: 12. "He shall divide the spoil with the strong." We have been delivered out of the hand of the destroyer, and we therefore belong to Him. His we are, and Him henceforth we serve.

WHAT IS IMPLIED IN OUR REDEMPTION

Leaving behind these picturesque descriptions of our salvation, we must own that we are the Lord's because of our redemption. If you turn back to the Old Testament in the book of Exodus, you will read the story of the deliverance of the Israelites from Egypt. This culminated in the great and awful night when the first-born in every Egyptian home was slain, but in every Israelite household, because of the promise of God and the blood of the Passover Lamb on the door, every first-born was secure. (Read in Exodus chapters 11 and 12.)

As a consequence of this protection of the first-born, they were regarded by God as belonging to Him. Exodus 13: 1 and 2, reads: "And the Lord spake unto Moses, saying, Sanctify unto me all the firstborn: . . . it is mine." In token of God's rights of possession of the firstborn, the institution of redemption money was inaugurated. You will read about this in Exodus 13: 11 to 16. In Numbers 3: 40-51, we find the interesting account of the substitution of the Levites as the property of God in the place of the firstborn of Israel. The fact that the firstborn of the Israelites were alive at all was due to their "redemption". They were the Lord's in a particularly significant way. The whole of the nation was thus symbolised by these redeemed firstborn, and likewise, belonged to the Lord.

GOD'S PERSONAL POSSESSION

Exodus 19: 4-5 reads, "Ye have seen what I did unto the Egyptians, and how I bare you on eagles' wings, and brought you unto myself. Now therefore, if ye will obey my voice indeed, and keep my covenant, then ye shall be a peculiar treasure unto me above all people: for all the earth is mine". The expression "for a peculiar treasure" means something that a man possesses for his personal use exclusively. The same term re-occurs in Malachi 3: 17, though in our English it is rendered "jewels". The thought is carried over into the New Testament, and in 1 Peter 2: 9, Christians are called "a peculiar people", or, as the Revised Version renders it, "a people for God's own possession". This is what we have seen already in Paul's expression in 1 Corinthians 6: 19: "Ye are not your own."

WE ARE BOUGHT WITH A PRICE

Look up in your concordance the words "redeemed" or "redemption", and "ransom". You will find them, for example, in Galatians 3: 13, in 1 Timothy 2: 6, in Ephesians 1: 7. All these passages and others, teach us that Christ has bought us for Himself. The Greek language has a very vivid way of showing the idea of doing something "for oneself", by a special form of the verb, and this is the form of the verb in some instances in these passages. Perhaps we may summarise this aspect of our relation to God by His own words: "This people have I formed for myself; they shall shew forth my praise" (Isaiah 43: 21).

The conclusion to be drawn from all this is that of our personal dedication. We should truly bear His name and recognise that it is written indelibly upon us. The exact meaning and derivation of the name "Christian" is "Christ's one". There is therefore but one attitude of mind for us all in the light of these great things. We must say with the apostle Paul at the time of his conversion, "Lord, what wilt thou have me to do?" (Acts 9: 6). Or we may use the words of the old-time prophet Isaiah, whose response to the call of God was, "Here am I; send me" (Isaiah 6: 8). This is the kind of dedication that must be made. Without any qualification or reservation in our hearts we must hold ourselves ready to do His will.

"IF THE LORD WILL"

James confronts us with this same obligation to recognise that we are the Lord's when he says, "Go to now, ye that say, To day or to morrow we will go into such a city, and continue there a year, and buy and sell, and get gain"; and then adds, "Ye ought to say, If the Lord will, we shall live, and do this, or that" (James 4: 13, 15). The supreme example for our behaviour in this respect is, of course, found in our Saviour's words at the time when the Cross drew so near to Him and when in Gethsemane He said, "Nevertheless not what I will, but what thou wilt" (Mark 14: 36).

Have you recognised this claim of Christ upon you? Do you really "belong" to Him? A friend of mine owned a motor car, but his frequent complaint was that he never had it. The reason behind this was that he had a nephew who was also very fond of the car, and whenever uncle William went to the garage he found it was empty, and learned that Neville had it. He paid the taxes and the insurance and all the up-keep; it was *his* car, and yet it was *not* his. We must see to it that nothing like this characterises our relation to the Lord.

The practical application of all this means all that follows and much more.

(1) *Your body is His.* Every part of you; your eyes, your voice, your ears, your hands, your feet; all belong to Him. "Keep thyself pure," said Paul to Timothy (1 Timothy 5: 22).

(2) *Your strength is His.* How appalling it is to see the strong going their own way, while the service of God is left to so many who are weak and frail in physique. Dedicate your strength to Jesus.

(3) *Your youth is His.* The vigour of youth, its zeal, its ambition, its enthusiasms: all these are needed in the work of God. Remember that the Saviour has redeemed your youth. Render it to Him therefore.

(4) *Your age is His.* You are an older person, and perhaps you have but recently come to a knowledge of Christ. In that case, the ripe experience of the years is something that belongs to the Lord. The Church needs the advice and counsel of those who are mature.

(5) *Your intellect is His.* Are you monopolising this for your business? Are you using it merely to attain some personal ends? Remember it is Christ's. Let your intellect work for Him. The work of the Gospel needs those who will "think" for Christ. It also needs the talents of business ability in its administration.

(6) *Your time is His.* We need a right view of time. Beware of the sin of "killing" time. It is sacred to Christ.

(7) *Your money is His.* For this, also, a right viewpoint is needed. All your money is God's. The practice of giving one tenth of our income is a good one in order to secure that necessary channelling of our money into the work of God, but we do not understand things aright until we acknowledge that *all* our possessions are His in the very first place.

(8) *Your talent is His.* To everyone of us God has committed some gifts, and these gifts are to be employed for

Him. Only one reputation matters, and that is the Lord's reputation.

(9) *Your heart is His.* This is the centre and, indeed, the solution of all. The Lord said to Simon, "Lovest thou me?" He wanted this affection first and foremost. Turn now to I Corinthians 3: 23, to a sentence that must ever be present in our minds throughout all our days, "Ye are Christ's".

"PRIVATE PROPERTY"—"TRESPASSERS WILL BE PROSECUTED". We might perhaps pair these two notices together, and remember that every time we ignore the truth that we belong to Christ we are really trespassing on that which is not our own. "I beseech you therefore, brethren, by the mercies of God, that ye present your bodies a living sacrifice, holy, acceptable unto God, which is your reasonable service. And be not conformed to this world: but be ye transformed by the renewing of your mind, that ye may prove what is that good, and acceptable, and perfect, will of God" (Romans 12: 1-2).

CHAPTER 14

Here is a practical question!

ARE THERE ANY INSTRUCTIONS?

Have you ever bought a mechanical object, such as a sewing machine, a type-writer, a motor car, or even less elaborate things? If so, you will have at once felt the need of some handbook or instruction book which tells you the way of the instrument. For the experiences of the Christian life we, likewise, have a book of instructions. This is nothing other than the Bible. When St. Augustine was stirred in his conscience and deeply in spiritual need, he heard a voice which spoke to him and said, "Take and read". God has given us a book, and this book—His Holy Word—constitutes our guide book for the way. It is "the greatest treasure this world affords".

THE APPEARANCE OF THE BIBLE

I hope you are not greatly perplexed by the appearance of your Bible. It looks at first as if it is so bulky. True, it is a large book, but not so large that it overwhelms us. Try to find your way round the Bible as soon as you can. Very often when you pick up a serious or useful book you consult the page which shows you the titles of the chapters. Looking in the front of your Bible you will find the list of "books" that it contains. This is immensely significant because the Bible is not one book; it is many. One old writer called it the "divine library".

THE DIVINE LIBRARY

You can imagine the books in this library as arranged on two shelves, thirty-nine on one—which we call the *Old Testament*—and twenty-seven on the other—which we call the *New Testament*. These books were written by thirty or forty different authors, and the writing was spread over a period of not less than fourteen hundred years. In spite of this immense variety of time and place and authorship, there is a wonderful *unity*. The Bible finds its unity in what it has to say to us about the ways of God. Do your best to learn the names of these books in the order in which they appear. You might think this to be a little uninteresting at first, but it will be an immense help to you to be able to find your way round the Bible speedily.

THE DIFFERENT KINDS OF BOOKS IN THE BIBLE

When you look into these books you find that some of them are books of history, some of them are books that describe religious practices, and some of them are sermons. You will discover a book which could be quite properly both prayer book and hymn-book—this is the book of *Psalms*, and you will find this a most useful book to turn to again and again. When you cannot find language to express your heart's desire, you will often find in the *Psalms* something that gives perfect vent to your feelings. In the second part of the book—the New Testament—there are the four records of the words and deeds of our Saviour which we know as the four Gospels, and these are followed by the "epistles", or letters, written by the Christian leaders to the early believers. A careful study of these books will build up your Christian knowledge and give you a greater understanding of what it is to be a Christian.

KNOW THE BOOK ITSELF

The supremely important thing for you at the beginning
of your Christian life is not to know a lot about the Bible,
but *to know the Bible itself*. It is a book for your life. When
Paul makes one of his greatest statements about the Scriptures by declaring their inspiration, he goes on at once to
say that they are "profitable for doctrine, for reproof, for
correction, for instruction in righteousness: that the man
of God may be perfect, thoroughly furnished unto all good
works" (2 Timothy 3: 16, 17). Here indeed is an instruction
book. It was the Psalmist who said, "Thy word have I hid
in mine heart, that I might not sin against thee" (Psalm 119:
11). When God referred to the unhappy experience of the
Israelites in the Old Testament, the only thing He could
say was, "O that thou hadst hearkened to my commandments! then had thy peace been as a river, and thy righteousness as the waves of the sea" (Isaiah 48: 18). The Bible is to
be enjoyed like food. Take its promises and use them to
nourish your faith. Use the Bible as our Lord did in conflict
with temptation. (See Matthew 4: 1-11, and note the words,
"It is written".) The evil one cannot stand against the sharp
point of this spiritual sword (Ephesians 6: 17).

HOW TO USE THE BIBLE

But perhaps you are still a little perplexed as to how to
use the Bible. Remind yourself all the time that it is a
book. There is nothing magical about it. There are no
mysterious ways of approaching it. You simply read it. It
is a mistake to pick out odd verses here and there very
much as you might in a "lucky dip" at a Christmas party!
You can understand the meaning of the words of the Bible
only as you read them in the light of what goes before
and what goes after. Habits of *daily* Bible reading therefore
should be formed by you from the very first. Some people
have adopted a slogan for themselves: "No Bible, no
breakfast."

HELPS FOR READING THE BIBLE

There is plenty of help that you can obtain these days to guide you in the reading of the Bible. There are organisations, which plan out a paragraph for every day. Usually short notes accompany the list of readings. Do not substitute the reading of the notes for the reading of the Bible; it is *the Bible* that matters.★

If you have the discipline of mind to do so, the very best way is to read a book at a time. I do not mean necessarily that you can read a whole book at a sitting, though this is by no means impossible in the case of most of the books of the Bible. It will be useful, however, to go consecutively through a Gospel, such as *Luke*, or a short epistle, such as *Philippians*, or a record, such as the book of *Genesis*. This will give you a broad view of the contents of a book. After that, you can adopt various methods of more detailed study; but whatever else is done by you, or is not done, this one thing you must do, you must read the Bible steadily.

VALUE OF THE BIBLE FOR LIFE

There is very much in the Bible that urges us to the careful and prayerful reading of it. After the death of Moses, God said to Joshua, his successor in leadership, "Only be thou strong and very courageous, that thou mayest observe to do according to all the law, which Moses my servant commanded thee: turn not from it to the right hand or to the left, that thou mayest prosper whithersoever thou goest. This book of the law shall not depart out of thy mouth; but thou shalt meditate therein day and night, that thou mayest observe to do according to all that is written therein: for then thou shalt make thy way prosperous, and then thou shalt have good success" (Joshua 1: 7-8).

At a time of religious awakening in the history of the

★The editors will be happy to advise on the choice of aids to Bible reading.

Old Testament, the great cause of the new spiritual life that came to the people is traced to a rediscovery—in a very literal sense—of the Bible. The temple had been in ruins, and when the builders went in to do the repairs the book of the Law was discovered. The reading of the book of the Law by the king and the people resulted in the cleansing of their lives as well as in the redecoration of the house of God. Read this thrilling story in 2 Kings, chapters 22 and 23. When the Bible came back to its central place, then the lives of the people were put right. This will be so for you and for me.

THE BIBLE POINTS US CONTINUALLY TO CHRIST

Our Lord said that Moses wrote of *Him*, and after His resurrection He talked with some of His disciples about this. He said, "These are the words which I spake unto you while I was yet with you, that all things must be fulfilled, which were written in the law of Moses, and in the prophets, and in the psalms, concerning me. Then opened he their understanding, that they might understand the scriptures" (Luke 24: 44, 45).

What harm we do ourselves by our forgetful neglect of this book of sacred instruction. "*Take, and read!*"

CHAPTER 15

Having taken to heart the importance of the instructions, we will set about

UNDERSTANDING THE BIBLE

You can understand the Bible only by studying it. The Bible is the greatest book in the world, and so we need not be surprised that it needs a lot of work to get to know it.

THE BIBLE IS CLEAR TO OUR HEARTS

In some ways the Bible is an easy book. It was intended by God to help those who are simple and earnest in their hearts. No one who wants to find his way to God could fail to do so by an honest reading of the Bible. Although it is perfectly true that there is much in the Bible which stretches our powers to the utmost, it is also true that the simple and pure in heart very often find their way about in the Bible much more surely than the sophisticated. Do you remember our Lord's words about the Heavenly Father's way of revealing things to "babes"? Look them up in Matthew 11:25. If you come to the Bible with an open heart and an open mind you will find much treasure.

THE BIBLE SHOULD BE READ THROUGH

The obvious first thing to do is to *read* the Bible. You may perhaps think that the Bible is such a big book that it will take you a very long time. The task is not so great as you fear. There are just under twelve hundred chapters in the Bible. This means that if you read about three and a half chapters a day you will have covered the whole Bible in one year. When you were in the habit of reading novels you read much more than this amount in one evening or in the train. Let me give you some practical advice about reading the Bible.

(a) Read! Read every day.

(b) Give at least as much time to it as you used to give to the newspaper and other books.

(c) Ignore all chapter and verse divisions (except in the case of the *Psalms*). Sweep your eye across the horizon and read on uninterruptedly.

(d) Do not stop to understand everything. Skip the genealogies (long lists of names).

(e) Refrain from writing anything at all at this point.

(f) Be prayerful in your reading, but do not think that "prayerful" means "magical" and that something mysterious is going to "happen" when you read. God's book has to be studied intelligently and will give its truth to the thoughtful mind.

METHODS OF BIBLE STUDY

In addition to this common-sense method of reading the Bible through, there are other and more particular ways of getting down to detailed study. The Bible can be studied in the following ways:

(1) Book by book
(2) Chapter by chapter
(3) Verse by verse
(4) Word by word

THE BEST METHOD FOR A BEGINNER

The best method for a beginner is to try to understand the Bible *book by book*. Take up such a short book as the First Epistle to the *Thessalonians* and read it through, say, a dozen times. You will be astonished at what comes about in your mind. The epistle will take hold of you, and its argument will carry you with it. Previously you have studied "texts" and have been unable to see the wood for the trees. There is no method of study more rewarding than book-by-book study. Many a difficult sentence or verse becomes much plainer when seen in the irresistible flow of the context.

It is in this way that the Bible is the interpreter of itself. "Every book in the Bible has an *object* as well as a *subject*" (Anstey), and this object will again and again provide us with the understanding of an obscure point. The thought of every orderly writer proceeds from stage to stage, and his material groups itself in some way. The titles that you find for the argument of the material will make the author's method and the course of his reasoning stand out quite clearly.

I THESSALONIANS

Let us take 1 Thessalonians once again as our example. The book falls into two.

    I. *A Personal and Historical section* (1: 2 to 3: 13).
    II. *A Practical and Doctrinal section* (4: 1 to 5: 24).

It is extremely important that you should make these divisions of the book yourself. What you do yourself is of infinitely greater value than what somebody else does for you. Under the main divisions you will frequently find it possible to make sub-divisions. Here are the sub-divisions of the first section of 1 Thessalonains.

  1. *Paul's Thanksgiving for the Conversion of the Thessalonians* (1: 2-10).
    (a) How they received the Gospel (2-7)
    (b) How they propagated the Gospel (8-10)
  2. *Paul's Vindication of his Thessalonian Ministry* (2: 1-16)
    (a) His exemplary life and labours (1-12)
    (b) Their sufferings for the Word of God (13-16)
  3. *Paul's affectionate Concern for the Thessalonian Church* (2: 17 to 3: 13)
    (a) His desire to revisit them (2: 17-20)

(b) The mission of Timothy (3: 1-8)
(c) Thanksgiving and prayer (3: 9-13)

If you will proceed by means of conscientious and slow hard work like this you will find that your understanding of the Bible will grow rapidly.

AIDS TO STUDY

There will, naturally, be points that do not come clear to you on your own first and simple reading of the Bible. You will, therefore, need a little help. There are many books today which enable the English reader to get to grips with some of the difficult places in the Scriptures. You will sometimes find it good to read what are known as modern English versions of the Bible. There is, of course, the Authorised Version, and then the well-known Revised Version, and now the New English Bible. These taken together will very often give you the help you need.

As soon as possible you should procure a concordance; it is a most valuable tool—indeed you cannot proceed very far in your study of the Bible without finding your need of one. A good English concordance sets out in alphabetical order all the words in the Authorised Version, and gives the reference in the Bible (book, chapter, verse) where the word occurs. The most famous and popular concordances are Cruden's, Strong's or Young's.

FIND CHRIST IN THE BIBLE

Is there anything to look out for in the Bible? Is there some idea running through the whole that gives a kind of clue to its meaning? There certainly is. Our Lord said about the writings of Moses, "*He wrote of me*" (John 5: 46). At the end of Luke's Gospel, in chapter 24, verse 27, we read that our Lord was talking to the two on their way to Emmaus, "And beginning at Moses and all the prophets, he expounded unto them in all the scriptures the things concerning himself". Our Lord Jesus is the clue to the meaning of the Bible. It has often been said the Bible is the *written*

Word of God, and Christ is the *living* Word of God. It is when we know the *living* Word of God that we may the more fully understand the *written* word of God.

A JIG-SAW PUZZLE

Some small children were on one occasion endeavouring to put together a complicated jig-saw puzzle. They were not succeeding very well. Suddenly one of them noticed on the reverse side of the pattern what appeared to be a portion of the face of a man, and exclaimed, "There's a man on the back!" They at once decided to turn all the pieces over and build up the face of a man—a comparatively simple task—and then reverse it in order to reveal the complicated pattern which they were finding it difficult to make. This is true about the Bible. There is a Man "behind the Book". When we know *Him*, we can find our way around the *Bible*, and the *Bible* in turn helps us to know *Him* better.

THE TWO PARTS OF THE BIBLE

You will have noticed that the Bible is divided into two main parts, the Old Testament and the New Testament. These two parts have their division at the point where the Lord Jesus came into the world. The Old Testament, therefore, points towards His coming, and the New Testament looks back upon it. We could say that in the Old Testament there is *Preparatory* Revelation, and in the New there is *Explanatory* Revelation.

THE MEANING OF REVELATION

By "revelation" is meant a "making known" or an "unveiling". God shows Himself to us in the Bible, and we are to seek to find God in the Bible. He has shown Himself in many ways. First of all, He has revealed Himself in the great movements of history, of which He has command. Further, He has shown Himself in many of those special indications of His will that He gave in the religious life of the Israelites and in the personal experiences of men and women of old times. The supreme revelation of God is in the Person of His Son. Jesus said, "He that hath seen me hath seen the Father" (John 14: 9), and the Bible gives to us the knowledge of our Lord Jesus Christ. Everything points to *Him*.

THE THEME OF THE BIBLE

We may, therefore, turn in our thinking to what we may call the "theme" of the Bible. The Bible is the Book of Salvation. Paul reminded Timothy that from a child he had "known the holy scriptures, which are able to make thee wise unto salvation through faith which is in Christ Jesus" (2 Timothy 3: 15). Let us think then of the Bible as the *Book of Salvation*. We may divide up its contents into six main portions.

(1) *The Need of Salvation*

This is shown to us in the opening book of the Bible. In the book of *Genesis* man is shown to have been made in the image of God, but then to have sinned. See Genesis, chapter 3. The Bible thus deals with man as a sinner.

(2) *The Foreshadowing of Salvation*

In the Old Testament we begin to learn of God's purpose to save man and deliver him from his adversary. This is revealed as early as Genesis 3: 15. We then find God beginning to work, and Noah finds grace in the eyes of the Lord (Genesis 6: 8). Abraham is chosen, and God makes His Covenant of Grace with him (Genesis 12: 1-3; 15: 1-21; and 17: 1-8). Through Moses God prescribes the sacrifices for sin and appoints the priesthood for sinners. For these great things you must read the books of *Exodus* and *Leviticus*. In the king David, God foreshadows the royal Saviour who was to come. In the repeated messages of the *Prophets*, God calls His people to repentance (Joel 2: 12-17), and in Isaiah 53 there is set forth, in the loftiest language the Old Testament knows, the saving work of the Lord Jesus as the One who "bare the sin of many" (Isaiah 53: 12).

(3) *The Effecting of Salvation*

This is the title that we may give to the *Four Gospels*. Here we have presented to us the birth, life, death, and resurrection of our Lord Jesus Christ. In John 19: 30 our Lord exclaims triumphantly, "It is finished". All that was needed for our salvation was effected by our Lord.

> He died that we might be forgiven,
>   He died to make us good,
> That we might go at last to heaven,
>   Saved by His precious blood.

(4) *The Proclamation of Salvation*

This is found in the book of the *Acts*—the book that gives us a record of the early preaching of the Gospel. Turn up and study such verses as Acts 2: 38; 8: 4; 16: 31; and 20: 21. In this last verse Paul affirms that the whole preaching of the Gospel may be summed up as "repentance toward God, and faith toward our Lord Jesus Christ".

(5) *The Unfolding of Salvation*

It is the great contribution of the *Epistles* of the New Testament that they unfold to us the meaning of our Saviour's work, and its application to our own lives. We are told, for example, that "Christ died for the ungodly" (Romans 5: 6); that there is now "no condemnation to them which are in Christ Jesus" (Romans 8: 1); that it is possible to be delivered from sin, and that the way of salvation is through faith in the Lord Jesus Christ (Galatians 2: 16).

(6) *The Consummation of Salvation*

In the last book of the Bible we hear the cry, "Behold,

I make all things new" (Revelation 21: 5). In the book of the *Revelation* we learn that "God shall wipe away all tears from their eyes; and there shall be no more death, neither sorrow, nor crying, neither shall there be any more pain: for the former things are passed away" (Revelation 21: 4).

This is the sixfold *Theme of the Bible*, and this sacred Book readily yields its treasures to those who humbly seek for them in dependence upon the Saviour of whom it speaks.

CHAPTER 16

If reading the Bible is listening to God as He speaks to us, prayer is our speaking to God. But

WHY SHOULD I PRAY?

First of all, do please remember that prayer isn't just "asking God for things". It is something very much bigger. The word describes our whole life with God. But let us stop a moment here and ask, "What is the life we have received as Christians?" Our Lord said, "I am . . . the life" (John 14: 6), and so the life that comes to us in Christ is none other than the life of God. Prayer, then, is the exercise of the life of God in us. If we get behind the scenes, as it were, we find it is something like the following. God by His Holy Spirit approaches us in the secret place of our hearts and then, by that same Holy Spirit, He creates desires in us for Himself. Our new life is life that comes from God and so needs to sustain itself by God. All its desires run towards God. We cannot therefore have the life of God within us without the experience of prayer.

We may think of this subject in another way, however. Because we have been born again, there is in us what there is in every child towards his parents, that is, a sense of sonship; and God who brought us to life by His Spirit makes us aware of the fact that we are His sons. This is what the New Testament calls the spirit of sonship. What son is he who never wishes to talk with his father? This would be the very denial of true sonship. The Spirit of God's Son given to us cries back to Him from our hearts, "Abba, Father" (Abba is an Aramaic way of saying, "My Father"), Galatians 4: 6. When our Lord was teaching the woman of Samaria at the well about the realities of the experience of God, He said, "God is Spirit, and they that worship him must worship him in spirit and in truth" (John 4: 24, R.V.). Alongside those words we have to note what our Lord had previously explained. He said, "The hour cometh and now is, when the true worshippers shall worship the Father in spirit and in truth: for the Father seeketh such to worship him" (John 4: 23). The One who is seeking the fellowship of His worshippers is none other than the "Father", and He longs that they shall worship Him "in spirit". Now what spirit can it be which a father seeks? Surely it is the spirit of a son who, because he loves his father, enjoys his company and speaks with him intimately and often. This is why we should pray: because we are sons.

Another of the prominent New Testament words for our experience of God is the word "fellowship". This is what John says in his First Epistle, chapter one and verse three. "Truly our fellowship is with the Father, and with his Son Jesus Christ." Fellowship means sharing together, and it is a word that is very warm with affection. Fellowship with the Father and with His Son is an expression of love. It is because the love of God has been shed abroad in our hearts by the Holy Ghost that we seek His face.

For all these reasons, then, we should pray.

ENCOURAGEMENT TO PRAY

If we want any encouragement for this, the greatest is certainly that which comes from the example of the Lord Jesus Christ Himself. Read the Gospels through and see how many times there is a reference to our Lord at prayer. He went away to quiet and lonely places to pray; He stayed up all night to pray; He arose a great while before day in order to pray (Luke 6: 12; Mark 1: 35). If He needed to pray, whose fellowship with the father was so pure and strong, how much more do we need to pray!

Not only have we the example of Christ, but we have also the inspiring words of the New Testament. We have the words that fell from our Lord's own lips and the words written down by the apostles. Our Lord taught that men ought always to pray and never to be discouraged in it (Luke 18: 1). The apostle Paul urged us to "pray without ceasing" (1 Thessalonians 5: 17). We are thus commanded to pray; and when a command coming from God coincides also with our deepest sense of need, how easy is that command to obey!

During the war a notice was chalked on a board outside a London church which read: "If your knees knock, kneel on them." This is the time to pray.

DIFFERENT KINDS OF PRAYER

Perhaps we must now look a little deeper into the nature of prayer. The idea of prayer is not exhausted in terms of having a "prayer list", very much as a woman has a shopping list when she goes out to the stores. Prayer is, of course, very much deeper than this, though there is no doubt that it certainly includes what the apostle Paul calls letting "your requests be made known unto God" (Philippians 4: 6). We have already been able to see that prayer is meeting with God; seeking Him face to face in order to know Him for Himself. Prayer is having to do with God, so that by the sense of His nearness we may be purified in our thoughts and strengthened in our hearts.

CONFESSION

If prayer is like this, it will inevitably mean that in our prayer time we shall be compelled to own up to God about our sins. We cannot meet with God very often without discovering how unlike Him we are, and as soon as we come into His presence the reflection dawns upon us that our behaviour at other times is so inconsistent with the purity and glory of communion with God. The confession of our sins will therefore find a large place in our approach to our Heavenly Father. Look at the prayer of Ezra in Ezra 9: 5-15 and of Daniel in Daniel 9: 3-19.

PRAISE

If nearness to God provokes in us a sense of unworthiness, and therefore of confession of sin, it will just as truly awaken in our hearts a sense of praise and gratitude. Has somebody ever done you a great kindness and you have forgotten it? Unexpectedly they come to see you, and as soon as you are with them you are at once reminded of your indebtedness to them and their generous action toward you, and you express yourself suitably. So it is between ourselves and God. No sooner do we come into His presence than there comes back to us the memory of His exceeding great goodness to us. Daily we are loaded with benefits, and true prayer is accompanied by thanksgiving and gratitude. See Psalm 103.

PETITION

We return in our thought, however, to the fact of our constantly recurring need of God. We are sinners still. We therefore need His restoring and upholding grace. We are the children of our Heavenly Father, and He knows what things we have need of before we ask Him. It was our Lord, however, who said, "Ask, and it shall be given you; . . . for everyone that asketh receiveth" (Luke 11: 9, 10). It is quite in place in our prayer, therefore, to pour out our hearts' needs before our Heavenly Father and to tell Him all our desires.

> Oh, what peace we often forfeit,
> Oh, what needless pain we bear,
> All because we do not carry
> Everything to God in prayer.

This is one of the great reasons why we should pray. "Ye have not, because ye ask not," said James (James 4: 2), and how poor we are simply for the want of asking! A small girl of a well-known American family was late home from school one day. It turned out that she had paid a formal call on Professor Einstein. Her father was much amused when he met the famous mathematician a few days later. "The reason your little girl called on me," explained the professor, "was to ask me to help her with her arithmetic lesson." And why not?

INTERCESSION

Intercession means praying for other people. This will have a practical effect upon us. We shall bring not only our own personal and family and business needs to God, but we shall make requests for others. We read that the Lord delivered Job from all his troubles "when he prayed for his friends" (Job 42: 10), and how often this is true in our times of prayer. When we cease dwelling on our own sorrowful complaints and begin to pray for others, how great is the relief of spirit and the enlargement of heart that comes. We are told to pray for one another (James 5: 16). This is a good thing to do. Pray for your parents, your husband, your wife, your children, your neighbours—and your enemies.

TWO FINAL PIECES OF ADVICE

Perhaps you are perplexed about the language of prayer. You have heard people use certain words and phrases which are unfamiliar to you. May I suggest that you do not try to learn such words and phrases? Speaking humbly and reverently, you should approach the Heavenly Father in words that exactly express your own heart's need. Let your heart talk. Study the Bible for such helpful prayers. Both the Old and the New Testament are full of stimulating examples. Supremely, of course, we have the Lord's Prayer, which every child of the Heavenly Father loves to use

(Matthew 6: 9-13; Luke 11: 2-4). Do not make it a "vain repetition as the heathen do", but nevertheless use it.

Above all else, remember the great promises of God which are annexed to prayer. Plead those promises. Be bold like David, who said to God on one occasion, "Do as thou hast said" (1 Chronicles 17: 23). Listen to the testimony of your own heart again and again as you are able to remind yourself of answered prayers in days that are already past. Pay heed to the testimony of others who likewise can tell you of the faithfulness of God in answered prayer.

Why should I pray? There is every reason to pray.

Chapter 17

Prayer is worship, and we may worship alone or in company with other believers. I want now to look into the question,

HOW TO WORSHIP GOD

Some go to church to take a walk;
Some go there to laugh and talk;
Some go there to meet a friend;
Some go there, their time to spend;
Some go there to meet a lover;
Some go there a fault to cover;
Some go there for speculation;
Some go there for observation;
Some go there to doze and nod;
The wise go there to worship God.

Worship is found everywhere. No tribe or nation has ever been discovered without some forms of worship. These forms have often been simple and elementary. Sometimes they have even been crude, distorted and revolting.

PAUL AT ATHENS

This latter is that ignorant "worship" to which Paul referred on one occasion (Acts 17: 23). He was visiting an exceedingly cultured city, the city of Athens. While he was waiting for his friends to arrive, he walked round the city and saw its temples, its shrines, its statues and its images. In the course of his walk one day, he came across an altar which was dedicated to the "Unknown God". A short while afterwards, when making a speech on Mars Hill—the "Speaker's Corner" of Athens—he opened his remarks with a kindly reference to their religious enthusiasm and referred to the altar with its inscription to the "Unknown God".

He proceeded at once to preach a sermon on God. "God that made the world and all things therein," he said, "seeing that he is Lord of heaven and earth, dwelleth not in temples made with hands; neither is worshipped with men's hands, as though he needed any thing, seeing he giveth to all life, and breath, and all things" (Acts 17: 24-25). He finished up his speech with another reference to this "ignorance" and made it plain that God "commandeth all men everywhere to repent" (verse 30). Read this most instructive story for yourself. It begins at verse 16 and goes on to the end of the chapter.

RIGHT IDEAS ABOUT GOD

It is obvious that for any worship to be acceptable and right there must be a knowledge of God and of the nature of His holy requirements. The first and fundamental thing is to have a right idea about God, and it is to this that we must turn our attention now. It is valuable to observe here that because the true worship of God depends upon His revelation of Himself that the reading and preaching of the Bible occupies such an important place in public worship.

It is impossible to have an idea of God that is too high. It is possible, however, to have an idea that is too theoretical. God is to be known in the way in which He has revealed Himself. He has shown His character, His strength, and His wisdom, in the experiences of those to whom He has made Himself known. We ought to note particularly two outstanding things which the Bible makes plain to us about God, namely, that God is the Creator and God is great.

GOD IS THE CREATOR

See Genesis 1: 1. How majestic is the language! "In the beginning God created the heaven and the earth." To pause here is to be confronted with an awe-inspiring thought.

The purpose of this chapter at the beginning of the Bible is not so much to give us a doctrine of creation, as a doctrine of God the Creator. This same truth is re-affirmed in the last book of the Bible in Revelation 4: 11, which reads, "Thou art worthy, O Lord, to receive glory and honour and power: for thou hast created all things, and for thy pleasure they are and were created". The whole of creation, in all its parts, and each part in its own way, is dependent on God. See the words again in Acts 17: 24, 26 and 28. God opens His hand, and satisfies the desire of every living thing (Psalm 145: 16).

GOD IS GREAT

"Greatness" is a word that combines those aspects of God's Being in which He is so infinitely exalted above us. The sin of the Old Testament people is summed up in an accusation which God brought against them when He said, "Thou thoughtest that I was altogether such an one as thyself" (Psalm 50: 21). Turn to Isaiah 40—the whole of the chapter—for a magnificent account of the greatness and glory of God, and then compare this with the words in Isaiah 57: 15, "For thus saith the high and lofty One that inhabiteth eternity, whose name is Holy; I dwell in the high and holy place, with him also that is of a contrite and humble spirit, to revive the spirit of the humble, and to revive the heart of the contrite ones".

OUR FATHER IS IN HEAVEN

When our Lord, who has brought us so near to God, taught us to pray, He put words into our lips which remind us that God is high above us: "After this manner therefore pray ye: Our Father which art in heaven, Hallowed be thy name" (Matthew 6:9). God's name is therefore to be held in reverence and honour, and He is to be approached with humility. God is not to be thought of as a kind of "Big Uncle" to whom anybody can run in any kind of trouble. It is true that He is ever approachable by the needy, but we must never allow ourselves to forget that He is on the throne. Turn again to the book of Isaiah and read chapter 6, verses 1-7, for another impressive account of God's greatness.

By the idea of God's greatness we shall indicate to ourselves the fact that He is (a) omnipotent, that is to say, there is nothing too hard for the Lord (Jeremiah 32:17). He is (b) omniscient, that is, there are no secrets hidden from His knowledge (Psalm 139:1-6). He is (c) omnipresent, that is, there is no place where we can be away from God (Psalm 139:7-12). He is (d), eternal, that is to say, He is not bound by the limitations of time, as we are, and although He is aware of things happening one after another, He also sees the end from the beginning. His mind is so different from ours that He sees the past, the present and the future in their completeness. Look up the following Scriptures: Psalm 90:2 and 4; Psalm 102:24-27; and Isaiah 40:28.

GOD'S PERFECT CHARACTER

With all these high qualities God is perfect truth, perfect wisdom, and perfect love. By His perfect truth we mean His utter reliability—His faithfulness, if you like. See the following passages: Deuteronomy 7:9; 32:4; 1 Corinthians 1:9; 2 Thessalonians 3:3.

By His perfect wisdom we mean His ability to plan and to control all things so as to fulfil His glorious purposes. See the following passages: Proverbs 3:19; 1 Timothy 1:17; James 1:5.

By His perfect love we mean that all that God does is directed to the blessing of those who trust in Him. See the following passages: John 3:16; 1 John 4:8 and 16; Ephesians 2:4 and 5; Romans 5:6-8.

In His greatness God is the Ruler of the whole universe and must be acknowledged as Lord over our consciences, our wills and our actions. The distinctive title which our Lord used when He spoke of God, that is the title "Father", sums up all these tender and strong qualities that belong to the "greatness" of God.

Paul was surely right when he exclaimed in Romans 11: 33-36, "O the depth of the riches both of the wisdom and knowledge of God! how unsearchable are his judgments, and his ways past finding out! For who hath known the mind of the Lord? or who hath been his counsellor? Or who hath first given to him, and it shall be recompensed unto him again? For of him, and through him, and to him, are all things: to whom be glory for ever. Amen."

TRUE WORSHIP

It can now be seen that to worship God aright we must grasp hold of these two things: God is our Maker and God is our Lord. Any worship which does not proceed on these lines must be false worship. Look up two passages which relate these truths about God to our ways of worshipping Him: Psalm 100 and John 4:22-24.

THE WORSHIPPER

We have not quite finished our brief study of "How to Worship God", for we have said nothing about the worshipper. We are the worshippers, but how can we worship? We are fallen and sinful men and women; our hearts by nature have a strange and bitter resentment against God; and we have broken God's holy Law and displeased Him in our hearts.

RELIGIOUS PERFORMANCES WILL NOT DO

It will not do to come to Him with the outward performances of worship alone. God expressed His distaste for this in the words of Isaiah 29: 13: "This people draw near me with their mouth, and with their lips do honour me, but have removed their heart far from me." (See Mark 7: 6.)

Look again at the words of Micah 6: 6-8: "Wherewith shall I come before the Lord, and bow myself before the high God? shall I come before him with burnt offerings, with calves of a year old? Will the Lord be pleased with thousands of rams, or with ten thousands of rivers of oil? shall I give my firstborn for my transgression, the fruit of my body for the sin of my soul? He hath shewed thee, O man, what is good; and what doth the Lord require of thee, but to do justly, and to love mercy, and to walk humbly with thy God?" None of these things by itself will do. (In these passages, of course, God is not contradicting His own instructions about these things, but merely protesting against their abuse.)

WHAT GOD SEEKS IN US

We must remind ourselves again of the words we have found in John 4: 24: "God is Spirit: and they that worship him must worship him in spirit and in truth." Examine also what David says in Psalm 51: 16-17, "For thou desirest not sacrifice; else would I give it: thou delightest not in burnt offering. The sacrifices of God are a broken spirit: a broken and a contrite heart, O God, thou wilt not despise".

WORSHIP IN THE NAME OF JESUS

Our only possible approach to God as sinners is through the sinners' Saviour. This is what our Lord meant when He said in John 14: 6: "I am the way, the truth, and the life: no man cometh unto the Father, but by me." It is echoed again in 1 John 2: 1: "If any man sin, we have an advocate with the Father, Jesus Christ the righteous." Worship in the name of Jesus is worship that recognises the "awful purity" of God, and confesses that sin is an offence to him. At the same time it is the worship of one who trusts in the mercy of God extended to sinners through the saving work of the Lord Jesus. Only as we come in this way are we truly coming as God's "sons", and "the Father seeketh such to worship him".

TWO IMPORTANT THINGS

To summarise all this, we may say that there are two basic things:
(1) Get your ideas right concerning God.
(2) Get your ideas right concerning yourself.
If these are right you will soon find that all the other practical problems of worship fall into their right place.

METHODS OF WORSHIP

Not all Christians worship God after the same manner, so far as externals are concerned. Some kneel to pray, others stand or sit. Some worship with the aid of a prayer-book, others without one. Some incline toward the use of a stately building with all its aesthetic suggestiveness and help, while others are hindered by the ornate and are satisfied with a plain building. You may let your mind rest assured that all these things are secondary, so long as there is nothing in your ways of worship which violates the commands of God, or which mars the simplicity and sincerity of your approach to Him. Then follow the way that helps you most. Remember what Thomas Watson, the Puritan, said, "Posture in worship is too often imposture".

CHAPTER 18

An important question that every newly-converted person ought to answer is:

SHOULD I JOIN A CHURCH?

It is not good for man to be alone. This was God's thought about man at the beginning (Genesis 2: 18), and it is still true that we are not fully "persons" unless we are sharing with others and communicating to them.

SPIRITUAL COMPANIONSHIP NEEDED

If this is so in natural life, it is all the more true in the deepest things of spiritual experience. In Christian life it is not good for man to be alone. God has made provision for fellowship, and we meet with it in the remarkable chapter that describes the beginning of the church—Acts chapter 2. Towards the end of this chapter we come upon words like these. "Then they that gladly received his word were baptised: and the same day there were added unto them about three thousand souls. And they continued stedfastly in the apostles' doctrine and fellowship, and in breaking of bread, and in prayers" (verses 41, 42). In verse 44 we come upon a sentence of great significance: "All that believed were together."

"TOGETHER"

There is a series of words running through this section at the end of the chapter, and it will be worth your while to underline them in your Bible. They are the following: "added", "fellowship", "together", "church". All of these words are highly suggestive of the companionship we are given in our experiences of the Lord Jesus Christ. Our question is, "Should I join a church?" The church is just this very thing that Acts chapter 2 describes. It belongs to Christian life. The church consists of believers who are walking together in the Christian way. Its members are trusting in Christ, seeking to become like Christ, and looking forward to being with Christ.

THE BEGINNING OF THE CHURCH

How did the Church begin? In one sense there was a "Church" in Old Testament times. Look up the words in Malachi 3: 16, "Then they that feared the Lord spake often one to another: and the Lord hearkened, and heard it, and a book of remembrance was written before him for them that feared the Lord, and that thought upon his name". Here is the very essence of fellowship in the things of God. We usually think of the Church, however, as beginning on the Day of Pentecost. See the story again in Acts chapter 2. This was the day when the Holy Spirit came very specially to weld together believers into the unity of one body in Christ.

This is a rather deep truth, but it is taught quite plainly in 1 Corinthians 12: 12 and 13. "For as the body is one, and hath many members, and all the members of that one body, being many, are one body: so also is Christ. For by one Spirit are we all baptised into one body, whether we be Jews or Gentiles, whether we be bond or free; and have been all made to drink into one Spirit."

PREACHING THE GOSPEL

The Jerusalem church began with the hearing of the preaching of the Gospel. It resulted in the faith of many who then came together in their common loyalty to the Lord Jesus. Most of these early members of the Christian

Church were Jewish by descent. Their place of worship was on some occasions in a private house (Acts 2: 46, Acts 12: 12), and on other occasions in a portion of the temple courts where various Jewish sects were permitted to gather (Acts 2: 46, Acts 3: 11).

Their organisation was simple. The apostles were the divinely ordained spiritual leaders, and seven men were appointed a little later to deal with material aspects of the Church's life (see Acts, chapter 6). Gradually the Church grew and spread from city to city until by the time the New Testament closes we find that there are Christian churches in a large number of cities of the Roman Empire. In our next chapter we shall study something more about the nature of the Church and its organisation, but it will be useful to draw attention to a point that has already appeared in the above description.

THE CHURCH MEANS "TOGETHERNESS"

The Church is one, that is to say, there is but one company of believers in the Lord Jesus Christ. This is what we mean by "The Church". It is obvious, however, that as all believers do not live in the same town or city there will be appearances of "The Church" in various localities. For these companies of believers we usually use the word in the plural and speak of "the churches". In trying to find an answer to this question about the helpfulness of joining a church, it will be best if we remind ourselves again of that "togetherness" which really constitutes the church.

You are familiar in your daily paper, or in your other reading, with the word "ecclesiastical". As you know, this refers to Church affairs. The word "ecclesiastical" comes from the Greek word which lies behind our word Church. It is an exceedingly interesting one. It is made up of two parts, and we may best look at it in this way. In olden days when a meeting of the town's people was to be held in any Greek city, a town crier would go round the streets, and his task would be to announce a meeting. The word that described the resulting meeting or coming together of the people is exactly the same as has come to be used for the idea of the Church.

CALLING THE PEOPLE TOGETHER

What the town crier did in effect was to call the people out of their houses that they might come *together*. This gives us a true idea of the word in our New Testament. The Church is a company of people who have been called out from the world, but at the same time they have been called together and into a living and joyous fellowship with one another.

FELLOWSHIP

Several times in the course of this chapter the word "fellow-ship" has been used. This word means "sharing together", or a "having in common". It implies first of all that there is something which may be shared. This, of course, is the blessing of the Gospel. Better still, we may say there is some One who is to be shared. This is the Lord Jesus Himself. But the word also implies that there are those among whom the sharing is experienced. You can see, therefore, that the Christian looks not only upward to the Saviour, but he looks out, right and left, toward his fellow-believers in Christ. He realises that he is not a solitary person—a kind of "Robinson Crusoe"—but is saved in the company of others.

REASONS FOR JOINING THE CHURCH

Should I join a church? Yes! Because I am not the only believer. Just as all the members of the body are mutually dependent upon one another, so also we who are members of Christ need one another for the full development of our experience (see 1 Corinthians 12: 14 to 27). We need active fellowship with other Christians. This will save us from our selfishness and will subdue our pride. It will also shield us from many temptations. Sharing together with others—

that is, joining a church—will bring an added richness to our spiritual experience. By the prayers of other people, by their example and influence, we shall be helped.

Think highly then of the Church of God. Speak well of it. In Acts 20: 28, Paul speaks of it as "The Church of God, which he hath purchased with his own blood". In Ephesians 5: 25 and 27, he writes that "Christ also loved the church, and gave himself for it; . . . that he might present it to himself a glorious church, not having spot, or wrinkle, or any such thing; but that it should be holy and without blemish". If Christ thought so well of the Church, we ought to do the same. Honour it therefore: serve it and join it.

THERE IS NOT A PERFECT CHURCH ON EARTH

Undoubtedly you will go a very long way if you want to find a "perfect" church. Remember, therefore, that you are not to seek for a company of people in whom there are no faults or failings. If ever you were to find such a company and were to join it, then probably your joining it would cause it to cease to be perfect! We join the church not merely for what we may obtain from it, but in order that we may contribute to it in the spiritual things that God has made known to us.

LEADERSHIP

The life of the church in any locality requires leadership. We are to honour those who have the rule over us in this respect. This is what Paul means in 1 Thessalonians 5: 12-13, where he tells us "to esteem them very highly in love for their work's sake". In 1 Timothy 5: 17, he says, "let the elders that rule well be counted worthy of double honour, especially they who labour in the word and doctrine". We have the same truth emphasised in the epistle to the Hebrews in chapter 13, verse 7: "Remember them which have the rule over you, who have spoken unto you the word of God: whose faith follow, considering the end of their conversation." This same thought appears likewise in verse 17: "Obey them that have the rule over you, and submit yourselves: for they watch for your souls, as they that must give account, that they may do it with joy, and not with grief: for that is unprofitable for you."

ACTIVITY

The life of the church can be sustained only by an active fellowship within it. This is the vivid impression that is given to us from the story told in Acts 2. It is delightful to learn in Acts 4: 23, about two of the apostles who had been imprisoned and had been subsequently released, that "being let go, they went to their own company". How immense was the peace that they found in being able to be among those who felt the same as they did!

In Acts 12, we come upon another sort of trouble that befell the Christian Church, but in the house of Mary, the mother of John, we read, "many were gathered together praying". Towards the end of the New Testament, in Hebrews 10, we have the strongest encouragement to "join the church". It reads in verses 24 and 25, "And let us consider one another to provoke unto love and to good works: not forsaking the assembling of ourselves together, as the manner of some is; but exhorting one another: and so much the more, as ye see the day approaching".

Yes! Join the church and put all you have into it, but make sure that it is one which is faithful to the Word of God in its teaching and practice.

CHAPTER 19

We must now examine the pattern of

CHURCH LIFE

First let us learn

HOW THE CHURCH BEGAN

The Christian Church came into existence on the Day of Pentecost. See Acts chapter 2. There was, of course, a company of devout believers in the Old Testament, and also during the days of our Lord's earthly ministry, but it was not until the time of the coming of the Holy Spirit on the Day of Pentecost that the Church in the full New Testament sense of that word came into being.

The disciples were told to await the coming of the Spirit, and we find in the opening verse of Acts 2 that they were all together in one place when the Holy Spirit came to them. Subsequent upon Peter's preaching, a great number of people believed, and the facts are set out plainly for us in verses 41 to 47 of this chapter. Note the following important facts. (1) There were those who received the word; (2) they were baptised; (3) they were added; (4) they continued in fellowship, which took the form of observing the Lord's Supper and prayer. When we look into the story more closely we find that most of these early believers were Jewish. This was of the nature of things, because the Church began in Jerusalem. The majority of them seem to have been poor, though not all of them. Their place of worship was in the public courts of the Temple (Acts 2: 46; Acts 3: 1 and 11) and in the house of Mary (Acts 12: 12).

ITS GROWTH

Starting at Jerusalem, the Church spread. This was exactly what was purposed by the Lord. He had instructed His disciples to preach the Gospel to every creature, and in Acts 1: 8, He says, "But ye shall receive power, after that the Holy Ghost is come upon you: and ye shall be witnesses unto me both in Jerusalem, and in all Judaea, and in Samaria, and unto the uttermost part of the earth".

WIDENING CIRCLES

When we watch the history recorded in the book of the Acts we find that it took exactly the same shape as this verse suggests. After spreading in Jerusalem and in Judaea, the Gospel was then taken to Samaria, see the story in Acts, chapter 8. From there it gradually spread to the uttermost parts of the earth. This is repeated by the spread of the Gospel through the missionary labours of the apostle Paul, first of all in Asia Minor, then in Europe. Such great cities as Antioch, Ephesus, Philippi, Corinth, Athens, Rome, became the centres in which the Gospel was established and the Church founded. Find the location of these in a good map.

ADMISSION OF CHRISTIANS WHO WERE NON-JEWS

With the growth of the Church to include non-Jewish believers, there arose a problem in some quarters as to the terms upon which these Gentile believers were to be received into Church life. Some who had been strictly brought up in Jewish circles were apparently wishing to insist that Gentiles should conform to Jewish practices, such as circumcision. Others, however, like the apostle Paul, were able to see that this would have reduced the Church to a mere sect of Judaism. This matter was prayerfully discussed by the early Christians in a great Council which is described in Acts 15, and there we read of the guidance of the Holy Spirit through which it was established that all that was required for membership of the Christian Church was to know the Lord.

Reflection on the immense growth of the Church leads us to the important question of its government.

THE WAY THE CHURCH IS TO BE GOVERNED

The government of the Church is, of course, completely under the Lord Himself. He is the Head of the Church (Colossians 1: 18), but the point on which we need clear understanding is how the Lord who is the Head of the Church exercises His rule within it. The Church is described in 1 Corinthians 12: 4-31 as a "body", and the individual believers are like the individual members of the body. Each one has his own function in the life of the whole.

THE EARLY LEADERSHIP OF THE APOSTLES

It is clear, however, that whilst every believer has a contribution to make to the life and activity of the Church, special provision needs to be made in the life of a community for its leadership. It was perfectly natural that in the very early days the twelve "apostles" should find this leadership in their hands. We do not read of the activity of many of these, though the New Testament gives special place to the work of men like Paul, Peter, John and James.

The apostles, by virtue of their unique position as eye-witnesses of our Lord, and as His initial followers, occupied a position of leadership. There was an authority attaching to them which was recognised in all the churches. Associated with the apostles were others, such as Timothy, Titus, Mark, Barnabas, and Silas, who represented them in this more general superintendence of the many churches. Paul refers to having "the care of all the churches" (2 Corinthians 11: 28).

In addition to this wide and general ministry in the government of the Church, it became necessary to appoint leaders over the local community. The government of a local church appears to have been two-fold: (a) there were those whose responsibility was spiritual, and (b) there were those whose duties were more particularly concerned with the church's material needs.

BISHOP, ELDER, PASTOR

There are three names given to the responsible officers of a local church in its spiritual things. These are the terms: (1) Bishop, (2) Elder (or presbyter), (3) Pastor. You will find references to these titles in Acts 20: 17 and 28; Philippians 1: 1; 1 Timothy 3: 1.

There is no doubt an historical reason for the rise of these titles. Gentile churches would take the familiar communities of their own cities as their model and would call their leaders by the name of bishop or "overseer"; while Jewish churches would naturally follow the pattern of the synagogue, which was familiar to them, and call their leaders by the name elder or "presbyter". The term pastor has special reference to the kind of work which the spiritual leader performs. A careful examination of these terms in the New Testament reveals that they are interchangeable. Compare again the use of them in Acts 20: 17 and 28, and also in Titus 1: 5 and 7, and 1 Peter 5: 1 and 2.

DEACONS

The title "deacon" which we find in Philippians 1: 1, and 1 Timothy 3: 8, applies to those whose ministry had to do with the material things of the church. This title does not occur in the book of the Acts, though there is every reason to think that the appointment of "the seven" recorded in Acts 6: 1-6, gives the foundation of this particular office in the church.

CHURCH GOVERNMENT TODAY

When we look at the church of the present-day it seems a little confusing at first, but the various types of church government which we find about us all have some contact with this New Testament pattern. It is for the individual Christian to seek whatever instruction he can on the point, in order to find out for himself which of the current methods of church government seem to him to come nearest to the New Testament pattern. Episcopal churches are governed by "bishops", who have powers extending over large areas. Presbyterian churches are governed by a body of "presbyters" or "elders", who likewise have jurisdiction over an extended area. The Methodist churches are similarly governed. Congregational and Baptist churches and the Assemblies of Brethren are more strictly locally governed through pastors or elders who belong to the community in any one place.

THE DOCTRINE OF THE CHURCH

It is plain from the record given to us in Acts 2 that at the founding of the Church doctrinal teaching was immediately given. This is what is apparent from Acts 2: 42, where we read, "they continued stedfastly in the apostles' doctrine". Possibly the confession of faith required from a believer was a very short one, but very soon, as we learn from Luke 1: 1-4, the story of the life and teaching and work of the Lord was taught and learned and repeated in a fixed form, like the learning of a catechism. In this way the facts of our Lord's ministry became carefully and thoroughly grasped.

When Paul writes to the Corinthians he says, in the first epistle, chapter 15, verses 1-4, that this preaching consisted of the emphasis on the death of Christ for our sins, and His bodily rising again on the third day. The way Paul alludes to this suggests that this was the generally received body of Christian doctrine. In verse 3 of the epistle written by Jude, he exhorts the Christians that they should "earnestly contend for the faith which was once delivered unto the saints". It is apparent throughout all the writings of the New Testament that the apostles are anxious to illuminate the minds of the Christians in every place about the great facts and doctrines of the faith.

In recent years it has become rather popular to imagine that a church can dispense with a doctrinal statement, but this was by no means the view of the New Testament churches, and we make a great mistake if we imagine that a church can exist for long or remain strong without a clear doctrinal foundation.

WHAT THE CHURCH DOES

The primary calling of the Church in its relation to the world is to preach the Gospel. Preaching therefore may be called the first ordinance of the Church. By "ordinance" we mean that which has been ordained or instituted by Christ the Head of the Church. This was His last command before ascending to the Father. This was obviously taken to heart by the apostles, and the New Testament is the witness to the tireless energy with which the Early Church preached the Gospel in every place.

TWO ORDINANCES OR SACRAMENTS

In addition to the ordinance of preaching, there are what are commonly called the two "sacraments". The word sacrament means "a sacred sign". These two sacraments are symbolical rites in which the spiritual meaning of our salvation is enshrined. The "word" preaches to the ear, and the "sacraments" preach to the eye. They are: (a) Baptism and (b) The Lord's Supper.

BAPTISM

Our Lord's command to baptise is found in Mark 16: 16, and Matthew 28: 19. It is exhorted by the apostles in Acts 2: 38; 10: 48; and 22: 16. It is recorded as practised by believers in Acts 2: 41; 8: 12; 16: 15 and 33; 18: 8; and 19: 5. It is well known, of course, that certain divergencies of practice have developed within the Christian Church in connection with this ordinance, and this is not the place to go into detailed comparison of these practices. It must suffice to say that Baptism is essentially the sign that the one baptised is a partaker of the blessings of the Gospel and a member of the Body of Christ.

THE LORD'S SUPPER

The Lord's Supper was instituted by our Lord. Accounts of this are given to us in Matthew 26: 26-28, and Luke 22: 19 and 20. Paul refers to it in 1 Corinthians 11: 23-25. All these passages should be read very carefully. 1 Corinthians 11: 26, points out that this ordinance is to be observed until the return of Christ. We find that the Church observed this ordinance regularly: see Acts 2: 42 and 46; 20: 7; 1 Corinthians 10: 16; 11: 27. It is given three names in the New Testament. In Acts 2: 42, it is called "the breaking of bread"; in 1 Corinthians 10: 16 "the communion", and in 1 Corinthians 11: 20, "the Lord's supper".

This ordinance serves as a reminder of the Lord. It proclaims His death (1 Corinthians 11: 26; Mark 14: 24); it points to a covenant (Matthew 26: 28); it sets forth the unity of all believers in Christ (1 Corinthians 10: 16 and 17); it is a joyous feast, as a Passover (Luke 22: 15). The action of eating and drinking symbolises our participation by faith in the benefits of the Lord's death.

EVANGELISTIC AND PRAYER LIFE OF THE CHURCH

In addition to the observance of these special ordinances, we find that the Church lived in the fellowship of prayer. It was engaged in busy evangelism. There was sympathetic care for the poor, and a firmly disciplined corporate life.

CHAPTER 20

No one lives the Christian life seriously without the question presenting itself:

WHAT ABOUT OTHER PEOPLE?

Who are the other people? The Jews of our Lord's day had very narrow ideas about the "other people" for whom they were to have any interest or care. In order to correct these narrow, bigoted and selfish ideas our Lord told the story of the Good Samaritan (Luke 10: 25-37). It answered the question, "Who is my neighbour?" But the answer assumed the form of instruction on true "neighbourliness". We are not to pick and choose in our relationships with "other people". All are equally important to God and deserving of our concern. Our responsibility is to be truly "neighbourly". "Other people," therefore, are just those with whom God brings us into contact in the ordinary days and ways of our life. They are the people in our homes, the people who live next door to us, the people whom we meet in the bus, in the shops, in our places of work, and in every other contact.

DO WE OWE THEM ANYTHING?

Have we any obligations towards these "other people"? There is no doubt about the answer to this question. If we are followers of the Lord Jesus Christ, we cannot possibly be without concern for others. We have the example of the

Saviour who came to seek and to save that which was lost (Luke 19: 10). "Ye know," says Paul, in 2 Corinthians 8: 9, "the grace of our Lord Jesus Christ, that, though he was rich, yet for your sakes he became poor, that ye through his poverty might be rich." We are His followers and, therefore, "other people" must be our concern.

AN OLD TESTAMENT STORY

The story is told in the Old Testament of a group of lepers who were starving. Because they were lepers they were unable to enter populated places. The nearby city had been encircled by a besieging army. This army had taken fright and had fled hurriedly, leaving food and stores behind. The lepers discovered this and began to eat and drink as they went into the tents one after another. Then they said one to another, "We do not well: this day is a day of good tidings, and we hold our peace: if we tarry till the morning light, some mischief will come upon us: now therefore come, that we may go and tell the king's household". You will find this story in 2 Kings 7: 3-16. We are somewhat in this position. The Good Tidings (that is what the word "Gospel" means) have been made known to us, and we owe it to "other people".

THE EXAMPLE OF PAUL

Paul was seized by the spirit of this when he said, "Woe is unto me, if I preach not the gospel!" (1 Corinthians 9: 16). In Romans 1: 14 Paul acknowledges himself to be a "debtor both to the Greeks, and to the Barbarians". In his deep concern for "others"—and in this case particularly his own fellow-countrymen—he said, "I say the truth in Christ, I lie not, my conscience also bearing me witness in the Holy Ghost, that I have great heaviness and continual sorrow in my heart. For I could wish that myself were accursed from Christ for my brethren, my kinsmen according to the flesh" (Romans 9: 1-3).

MOSES

This same spirit had been voiced by the great-hearted Moses who, when his people had sinned a great sin, cried to God and said, "Yet now, if thou wilt forgive their sin—; and if not, blot me, I pray thee, out of thy book which thou hast written" (Exodus 32: 32).

ANDREW

We have some excellent examples in the Gospel story of personal evangelism of this kind. If you open the Fourth Gospel in chapter 1 at verses 40-42 you will read the story of Andrew who, having come to know Christ, went out immediately to find his brother, Simon, "and he brought him to Jesus".

> Find another, find another,
> Just as Andrew found his brother;
> I another soul would bring
> To the feet of Christ my king.

PHILIP

Philip was of the same spirit, for having heard the Lord's call "follow me", we read next that "Philip findeth Nathanael, and saith unto him, We have found him, of whom Moses in the law, and the prophets, did write, Jesus of Nazareth, the son of Joseph. And Nathanael said unto him, Can there any good thing come out of Nazareth? Philip saith unto him, Come and see" (John 1: 45-46).

THOSE WHO HAD BEEN BLESSED BY CHRIST

"Go home to thy friends, and tell them how great things the Lord hath done for thee, and hath had compassion on thee." This is what the Lord said to the man out of whom He had cast the devil (Mark 5: 19). The woman of Samaria needed no such instruction, but, leaving her water pot by the side of the well, she went into the town and said to the men, "Come, see a man, which told me all things that ever I did: is not this the Christ?" (John 4: 29).

It is a most profitable study to go through the book of the Acts and see the immense amount of personal witness which the Holy Spirit inspired in the hearts of the early Christians. It is particularly striking to notice in Acts 8: 4 that the "rank and file" of the church members, being scattered abroad from Jerusalem, "went everywhere preaching the word". The chapter continues with the story of Philip (not the one of whom we read in the Gospels), who, after being in a time of great blessing in the city of Samaria, was directed by God to go to a desert road in order to find one man and lead him to the Saviour.

IT IS ONE–BY–ONE

Personal—one-by-one—work seems often lacking in the glamour that belongs to the big evangelistic meeting, but Spurgeon once advocated personal work in the following way. He said, "If you had one hundred empty bottles before you, and threw a pail of water over them, some would get a little in them but most would fall outside. If you wish to fill the bottles, the best way is to take each bottle separately and put a vessel full of water to the bottle's mouth. That," he said, "is successful personal work."

SOMEONE WAS CONCERNED ABOUT ME

A lady visiting in a minister's family was told of some bright, cultured people in the neighbourhood, who, however, never attended any religious services. "I will go and see them," the visitor volunteered. "But what excuse will you have for going?" the hostess questioned anxiously. "Oh, yes; take this book. I remember having heard one of the young ladies express a desire to read it." "But I don't want an excuse," was the reply, "I want them to know I am interested in them." As a result of the visit, every member of the family became a regular attendant at the church service, and three of them became Christians. Speaking of it afterwards, the mother said: "I never realised the danger we were in till I saw that someone else—and that one almost a stranger—was concerned about me."

SUCH WERE SOME OF YOU

One of the strong motives that will help us in caring for other people is to keep ourselves reminded that we were just as they are until the Lord met with us and saved us. In I Corinthians 6, Paul has been giving a list of very evil sins, and he finishes by saying that the doers of these things shall not inherit the kingdom of God. He does not leave it there, however, for he goes on to say "and such were some of you". (1 Corinthians 6: 11). How salutary and humbling it is to realise that apart from the grace of God we should still have been in the same lost condition as "other people". We have to look at many a wandering sinner and then say, "but for the grace of God there go I".

> Lord lay some soul upon my heart,
> And love that soul through me;
> That I may nobly do my part
> To win that soul for thee.

GOD CAN HELP US IN THIS

We need our Lord's compassion on the multitudes. We need His devotion to the one lost sheep, which He illustrates in the parable (Luke 15: 1-7). We need His infinite sympathy and gentleness, such as He also illustrated in the story of the father who received back his prodigal son (Luke 15: 11-32). The work of reaching "other people" needs much wisdom, and we shall do well to learn from those who have had some experience of this. We need patience; we need guidance from God that we may give to those whom He has made ready; we need humility that we do not make ourselves offensive; we need prayer so that the tones in which we speak shall truly represent the spirit of Christ. He who is the great Shepherd of the sheep, however, will give us all the wisdom we need.

143

Change the picture. Our Lord said to the fishermen of Galilee, "Come ye after me, and I will make you to become fishers of men" (Mark 1: 17). Remember the words of James, "Let him know, that he which converteth the sinner from the error of his way shall save a soul from death, and shall hide a multitude of sins" (James 5: 20).

> Oh! for a heart that is burdened,
>   Infused with a passion to pray;
> Oh! for a stirring within me,
>   Oh! for His power every day;
> Oh! for a heart like my Saviour,
>   Who being in agony prayed;
> Such caring for others, Lord give me,
>   On my heart let the burden be laid.

CHAPTER 21

We Christians have a great hope

WHEN WE DIE

Nevertheless, death is *unnatural*. It is true that sometimes the acute physical pain of a terrible illness makes the sufferer ready to welcome death, but this is a circumstance of overwhelming strain where the judgment of the mind is not perfectly itself. Others, it is true, have sought to develop a stoic self-control in which they profess to have made themselves indifferent to death and appear to face this solemn reality without any qualms. These are instances where man's natural sensitiveness to the fine things of the spirit have become deliberately obliterated, and so once more the man who puts himself into this state of mind is abnormal. Every healthy-minded person shrinks from the thought of death. It does not truly belong to the purpose of our existence.

A FIGHTER PILOT

The following conversation occurred in the canteen at one of the air stations of the R.A.F. during the last war. A Christian officer was sitting at his meal, when into the canteen came the most fearless and most admired of the fighter pilots of the unit. After a short while the pilot addressed the officer and said how deeply he wished he were like him. The conversation had been on the subject of the dangerous nature of the tasks in which they were employed, and the young pilot confessed that he was afraid to die. The Christian officer replied that this was surely astonishing, because he was well known to be the most daring and obviously "unafraid" of men. To which the young pilot replied that it was not the "dying" part that he feared. He did not mind coming down in flames, he did not mind being shot through, he did not mind an explosion in mid-air; these things did not terrify him: it was the thought of *what was to come afterwards* that troubled him. This honest confession of a brave young man takes us nearer to the heart of this question than all the twisted notions of those who have tried to reason away from this solemn reality.

CHRISTIANITY IS REALISTIC

One of the outstanding things of Christianity is that it refuses to take death lightly. This is not because Christianity is a miserable affair, dwelling on gloomy subjects: it is because Christianity is *realistic*. Being realistic, Christianity recognises that death is an interference and that, therefore, the only way of real satisfaction for the desires that belong to human life is that death should in some way be conquered.

WHAT IS DEATH?

All kinds of definitions have been given of death, each one emphasising an important aspect. Perhaps it will be better for us not to seek a definition in formal terms, but rather to glimpse at some of the words which the Bible uses to describe it. In Joshua 23: 14, it is called "going the way of all the earth". This, of course, refers to the fact that *everybody* dies. In Deuteronomy 32: 50, we have the phrase, "gathered unto thy people", and in Judges 2: 10, the words "gathered unto their fathers". These suggest that when the soul leaves the body and the man is what we call "dead", he has gone into another realm—*a realm into which his forefathers had already entered.* In Ecclesiastes 12: 7, we come upon a rather more formal account of death in the words "Then shall the dust return to the earth as it was: and the spirit shall return unto God who gave it".

Turning to the New Testament, we find Paul speaking in 1 Thessalonians 4: 14, about those who "sleep" in Jesus. This is a description of the *bodily apearance* of those who have died. The body is, as it were, sleeping. It is inactive and not registering experiences through any of its senses. In 2 Corinthians 5: 8, Paul speaks about being "absent" from the body, and as an old man writing in 2 Timothy 4: 6, he speaks of "the time of *my departure*". From this brief survey of some of the Biblical phrases we gain some idea of what death is to a human being. We are not concerned with the merely biological or chemical meaning of death, but rather with the significance of it for living persons.

MAN LIVES ON AFTER HIS BODY HAS DIED

It is clear from the phrases that we have quoted that man is both material and immaterial, that is to say, he is body and he is spirit (soul is simply another name for an individual human "spirit"). At death the body ceases to function. It first of all ceases to breathe, and then all the other operations immediately come to an end. A disintegration sets in which the Bible calls a return to "dust". It is clear, however, that this is not the end of the man, for *he* lives on. He goes away, but he does not cease to exist. We face, therefore, the clear truth of an after-life, and it is upon this that we enter when we die.

THE AFTER-LIFE

Some have tried to deny the existence of such an after-life, but none of the arguments against it is convincing, while, on the other hand, it is unthinkable and completely irrational to conclude that when a man's body perishes all those other qualities in him that distinguish him from the beasts should likewise be extinguished.

147

The arguments in favour of the after-life are many. The *justice of God* seems to provide one of these. The *human conscience* demands some future life in order to satisfy it. See Psalm 73 : 16 and 17. It is a *world-wide conviction* that the soul of man survives after death, and there is no reliable record of a tribe or nation or religion in which some form of after-life is not assumed. The *incompleteness* of this life calls for another sphere in which man may experience the realisation of all that is within him. There are *ideals and desires* for which this present life seems to make no provision, and we cannot think that God is the author of a gigantic "frustration".

CHRISTIAN CONVICTIONS

But we are Christians. We do not need to base our thoughts on human speculation, or even the best of logical arguments. We have the revelation that God has given to us. Although it is true that the Old Testament contains no formal teaching about the life after death, we can see certainties of this continually breaking through the Old Testament record.

OLD TESTAMENT PASSAGES

First of all, the references to being gathered to one's fathers indicate this. The hope of the Psalmist in Psalm 16: 8-11, is that God will not *leave* his soul in hell. (The word here used is not the one that indicates final punishment: it is the word "Sheol" and is the name for the world of the departed in the Old Testament.) This provides us with another indication of the reality of the after-life. In Psalm 49: 15, the Psalmist says, "God will redeem my soul from the power of the grave", while the famous words of Job 19: 25-27, show that even though Job's body should perish and he himself should disappear from the earth, yet after all this he would see the Lord as his Vindicator.

IN THE NEW TESTAMENT

When we turn to the New Testament we find a great

amount of material establishing the reality of the after-life. It is made plain that there is an after-life, not only for the righteous, but also for the unrighteous. Look up such passages as:

(a) *After-life of the righteous:* Luke 23: 43; John 11: 25, 26; John 14: 2; Acts 7: 59; 2 Corinthians 5: 1-4.

(b) *After-life of the unrighteous:* Matthew 11: 21-24; 12: 41; Romans 2: 3-11.

As a final thought for us to notice in this brief study we must remind ourselves that all that the Gospel teaches about the resurrection is likewise a confirmation of the reality of the next life.

THE SOLEMNITY OF DEATH

The meaning of death for the unbeliever is serious. Death determines every man's destiny. This is the fact that is illustrated in the parable of the Rich Man and Lazarus in Luke 16, especially in verse 26. The same truth is made plain in Hebrews 9: 27, where we read, "It is appointed unto men once to die, but after this the judgment".

DEATH IS TRANSFORMED FOR THE CHRISTIAN

For the Christian believer, however, death is completely transformed. He still has to pass through the physical aspects of death. This is because of the corrupted nature of the body, which is one of the consequences of sin, but the effect of death is completely altered for the believer. Paul says in Philippians 1: 21-23, "To die is gain . . . to depart, and to be with Christ". He triumphantly exclaims in 1 Corinthians 15: 55, "O death, where is thy sting?" The sting of death has been removed by the Saviour who received it into Himself. This is the meaning of the words in Hebrews 2: 14 and 15; "Forasmuch then as the children are partakers of flesh and blood, he also himself likewise took part of the same; that through death he might destroy him that had the power of death, that is, the devil; and deliver them who through fear of death were all their lifetime subject to bondage".

THE BELIEVER HAS ALREADY "DIED"

The harmlessness of death in the personal experience of the Christian believer is found to reside in the fact that he has already passed through it. John 5: 24, says that he has "everlasting life, and shall not come into condemnation; but is passed from death unto life". It is this that lies deep in the saying of the Lord at the time of the death of Lazarus when in John 11: 26, He declared, "whosoever liveth and believeth in me shall never die". He does not mean by this that the body will not pass through death, but that death in all its awfulness will not touch the believer.

THE INTERMEDIATE STATE

The question is sometimes asked, "Where do we go when we die?" The word "where" is perhaps a little misleading, because we have no ideas at all of space and position in a world of spiritual existence. The New Testament, however, gives us some light on the matter in what it tells us about the intermediate state, that is to say, the state of personal experience between death and the final resurrection.

THE STATE OF THE UNGODLY

The state of the ungodly and the sinner in this "intermediate" condition is described as being in "Hades". This word seems to stand in the New Testament for that condition of sinners after they have left this life and while they await the judgment. In many ways the experiences of "Hades" are a kind of foretaste of the solemnities of the ultimate judgment which the Biblical word "Hell" represents. Luke 16: 23, gives us a pictorial representation of this suffering. In 1 Peter 3: 19, these departed spirits are said to be "in prison", or more literally, "under guard". This is repeated in 2 Peter 2: 9.

150

NO SECOND CHANCE

There is no truth whatever in the speculation of a "second chance". The Scripture represents the state of unbelievers after death as a fixed one. This receives confirmation in the parable of Luke 16: 19-31, and also in the words of John 8: 21-24, where a kind of finality seems to reside in our Lord's words, "Ye . . . shall die in your sins ". Further, we are told that the final judgment is determined by things done in the flesh, not by anything that happens afterwards.

BUT WHAT HAPPENS TO BELIEVERS?

The intermediate state of believers is represented by the word "Paradise". In effect this means that the believer enters immediately upon the blessed experiences of his redemption. He is said to be "present with the Lord" (2 Corinthians 5: 8), or, as Paul puts it in Philippians 1: 23, it is "to be with Christ". Our Lord gave this assurance to the dying thief in Luke 23: 43: "Today shalt thou be with me in paradise." We must be careful to think of the word "paradise" as indicating not so much a place but a state; it is a joyous condition—note the words "far better" (Philippians 1: 23). At the same time it is an incomplete condition: see the words in 2 Corinthians 5: 3 and 8; Romans 8: 23; and Philippians 3: 11. The receiving of a glorified body is the crown of our redemption and brings the intermediate state to an end in the glorious consummation of heaven itself.

UNIVERSAL RESURRECTION

We conclude our study by a final note on the fact of the resurrection. There is a universal resurrection at the "end". It includes the righteous and the wicked. Carefully examine the passages in Daniel 12: 2; John 5: 28-29; Acts 24: 15; Revelation 20: 13-15.

CHAPTER 22

This final chapter looks onward to

THE NEXT TIME MEN SEE JESUS

The world did not see the last of Jesus when it crucified him. Undoubtedly men like Caiaphas, and possibly also Pilate, thought that their troubles were over when once Jesus was crucified and the clamorous mobs had been dispersed. They expected that His few disciples would hide away in their villages in Galilee and return to their fishing and other normal ways of life.

THE CROSS WAS NOT THE END

But the Cross was not the end. It was our Lord's great triumph that ushered in far greater things than had been possible before. The powers of evil were broken at the Cross. "Having spoiled principalities and powers, he made a show of them openly, triumphing over them in it" (Colossians 2: 15). The Cross was followed by the Resurrection.

> Death cannot keep his prey—
> Jesus, my Saviour!
> He tore the bars away—
> Jesus, my Lord!

Up from the grave He arose,
With a mighty triumph o'er His foes;
He arose a Victor from the dark domain,
And He lives for ever with His saints to reign!
He arose! He arose!
Hallelujah! Christ arose!

THE EXALTATION OF JESUS

The resurrection of our Lord, confirmed to His disciples by his visits to them, was followed by His exaltation. After forty days (Acts 1: 3) our Lord ascended into heaven. Luke 24: 51, reads "And it came to pass, while he blessed them, he was parted from them, and carried up into heaven". This is again noted in Acts 1: 9, which is as follows: "And when he had spoken these things, while they beheld, he was taken up; and a cloud received him out of their sight."

The ascension was for our Lord a going back where He was before (John 6: 62). It meant for Him that the Father would glorify Him with the glory which He had with Him before the world was (John 17: 5). At His ascension our Lord was elevated to the throne of God. In Hebrews 1: 3, we read, "Who being the brightness of his glory, and the express image of his person, and upholding all things by the word of his power, when he had by himself purged our sins, sat down on the right hand of the Majesty on high".

Paul wrote the same truth in Philippians 2: 9 to 11, "Wherefore God also hath highly exalted him, and given him a name which is above every name: that at the name of Jesus every knee should bow, of things in heaven, and things in earth, and things under the earth; and that every tongue should confess that Jesus Christ is Lord, to the glory of God the Father". We are correct, therefore, in thinking of our Lord as highly exalted, reigning in glory, sitting on His Father's throne, "henceforth expecting till his enemies be made his footstool" (Hebrews 10: 13).

A great event is still to occur, however. Our Lord is yet to reap the glorious harvest of His triumphant Cross. This He will do at His Second Coming. Our Lord is to return. Have you ever said "Good-bye" to somebody with the sinking feeling in your heart that you will never see that person again? If so, you will know just what that experience is like. If, however, there is even the faintest hope of seeing your friend again, what a difference it makes to your feelings! With regard to the Lord Jesus Christ, there is far more than a "faint hope" of His return. It is clearly indicated. The plain statement of Scripture is that He who came to the earth in the lowly manger at Bethlehem will come again in the clouds of glory. This is what we mean by the Second Advent.

WHAT DID OUR LORD SAY ABOUT IT?

Did Jesus ever say anything about this? He did. In John 14 there is the record of an intimate talk which He had with His friends and disciples before He left. In verse 3 of that chapter He says, "I will come again".

THE COMING AGAIN IN GLORY

The word "come" on the lips of Jesus appears in the Gospels to have been used in a number of ways, but there can be no doubt that the most prominent meaning and use of this word by our Lord Jesus has reference to His final coming in the "clouds of heaven". The parables which our Lord told of the Servant and his Lord (Matthew 24: 45-51; Mark 13: 34-37), of the Ten Virgins (Matthew 25: 1-13), of the Talents (Matthew 25: 14-30), and of the Pounds (Luke 19: 12-27), all demonstrate the fact that He taught that He was to return in power and triumph. In addition to this parabolic teaching, there are the direct words of the Lord, as for example in Matthew 24: 30: "They shall see the Son of man coming in the clouds of heaven with power and great glory."

The rest of the New Testament takes up this same glad assurance. The two men in white apparel had said to the apostles, "Ye men of Galilee, why stand ye gazing up into heaven? This same Jesus, which is taken up from you into heaven, shall so come in like manner as ye have seen him go into heaven" (Acts 1: 11).

This assurance of our Lord's Second Advent found a firm place in the apostolic preaching from the very beginning. The epistles to the Thessalonians which are usually held to be among the earliest of Paul's writings, are concerned with this. Paul writes, "The Lord himself shall descend from heaven with a shout, with the voice of the archangel, and with the trump of God: and the dead in Christ shall rise first: then we which are alive and remain shall be caught up together with them in the clouds, to meet the Lord in the air: and so shall we ever be with the Lord" (1 Thessalonians 4: 16, 17). The Epistle to the Hebrews contains the same strong certainty. It reads, "So Christ was once offered to bear the sins of many; and unto them that look for him shall he appear the second time without sin unto salvation" (Hebrews 9: 28).

A GLORIOUS HOPE

The blessing and joy of our Lord's Return is beyond the power of human language fully to describe. That glorious return is the hope of the Church, and the climax of the spiritual expectation of the individual believer. "Beloved," wrote the apostle John, "now are we the sons of God, and it doth not yet appear what we shall be: but we know that, when he shall appear, we shall be like him; for we shall see him as he is. And every man that hath this hope in him (that is, in Christ) purifieth himself, even as he is pure" (1 John 3: 2, 3).

THE GREAT CLIMAX OF THINGS

The Second Coming of our Lord will bring to a triumphant conclusion the things He achieved on the Cross. It will mean the gathering of the spoils of that victory which was so gloriously won at Calvary. This is the meaning of the words in Hebrews 12: 2, where it is said that it was "for the joy that was set before him" that He "endured the cross". In Philippians 2: 8-10, we are again taught that it is because our Lord became obedient unto death, "even the death of the cross" that God has highly exalted Him, and given Him a name "which is above every name".

THE REMEMBRANCE OF THIS IN THE LORD'S SUPPER

Because the Lord's Return is the supreme hope of the Church and of the individual believer, and because it is our Lord's triumphant vindication of Himself and the reaping of the harvest of His sorrow, there is a very close association between the Lord's Supper and the Second Advent. In 1 Corinthians 11: 26, Paul reminds the believers that as often as they observed this sacred ordinance they would "show the Lord's death till he come".

How good a resting place is this! Let our hearts and minds but settle here, and we shall find the answer to all our human misgivings. He says, "I will come again" (John 14: 3).

TESTING OF BELIEVERS

There are other consequences of our Lord's Second Coming beside the immense comfort and consolation that this glorious hope gives. The next time men see Jesus will be the occasion of *discriminating judgment*. For Christians this will be the time when their work will be tested (see Romans 14: 10-12; 1 Corinthians 3: 9-15; 4: 5). Rewards will be given. Paul says in 2 Timothy 4: 8, "Henceforth there is laid up for me a crown of righteousness, which the Lord, the righteous judge, shall give me at that day: and not to me only, but unto all them also that love his appearing". This is endorsed by Peter in 1 Peter 5: 4, "And when the chief Shepherd shall appear, ye shall receive a crown of glory that fadeth not away".

THE LAST JUDGMENT

For the ungodly, the Second Coming of our Lord will bring the Last Judgment. No one will be exempt from seeing Him. Revelation 1:7, reads, "Behold, he cometh with clouds; and every eye shall see him, and they also which pierced him: and all kindreds of the earth shall wail because of him. Even so, Amen". The great judgment which is described in Revelation 20: 11-15, will then take place. Upon those who have rejected and resisted God there will be poured out the Divine vengeance, "in flaming fire taking vengeance on them that know not God, and that obey not the gospel of our Lord Jesus Christ: who shall be punished with everlasting destruction from the presence of the Lord, and from the glory of his power" (2 Thessalonians 1: 8 and 9). How exceedingly solemn are these words!

NEW HEAVENS AND NEW EARTH

The ultimate issues of our Lord's Return are found in the *new heaven and the new earth*. In 2 Peter 3: 11-13 Peter asks, "What manner of persons ought ye to be . . . looking for and hasting unto the coming of the day of God, wherein the heavens being on fire shall be dissolved, and the elements shall melt with fervent heat? Nevertheless we, according to his promise, look for new heavens and a new earth, wherein dwelleth righteousness". This is endorsed in Revelation 21: 1, where John tells us, "And I saw a new heaven and a new earth: for the first heaven and the first earth were passed away; and there was no more sea".

WHEN IS IT TO BE?

The exact *time* when they will next see Jesus is not known by men. Our Lord made this plain in Matthew 24: 36 and 42: "But of that day and hour knoweth no man, no, not the angels of heaven, but my Father only. . . . Watch therefore: for ye know not what hour your Lord doth come." He explained in Luke 17: 26-30 that men would be so preoccupied with their daily pursuits that they would be quite unprepared for the sudden and unexpected appearance of the Lord.

We are warned in the New Testament that before our Lord returns there will be a great increase of wickedness. In 2 Thessalonians 2: 3-4, we have the following words, "Let no man deceive you by any means: for that day shall not come, except there come a falling away first, and that man of sin be revealed, the son of perdition; who opposeth and exalteth himself above all that is called God, or that is worshipped; so that he as God sitteth in the temple of God, showing himself that he is God". This is what Paul likewise said to Timothy in 1 Timothy 4: 1 and 2, and 2 Timothy 3: 1-5.

THE IMPORTANCE OF BEING READY

Are you ready for the next time men see Jesus? We all must take to heart the warning that the Lord Himself gives, "Therefore be ye also ready: for in such an hour as ye think not the Son of man cometh" (Matthew 24: 44).